WILLIAM FORSYTHE

Choreography and Dance
2000, Vol. 5, Part 3, pp. iii–iv
Photocopying permitted by license only

Contents

Choreography and Dance
2000, Vol. 5, Part 3, pp. 1–7
Photocopying permitted by license only

Nijinsky's Heir: A Classical Company Leads Modern Dance

Senta Driver

The real founder of modern dance was arguably Vaslav Nijinsky, who presented new movement vocabularies and new structural models in the repertory of the Diaghilev Ballets Russes, which was generally understood to be a ballet company. Some viewers compared Balanchine's company to a modern dance organization for its unusual focus on one artistic vision and a decisively original movement philosophy. Seen in this light William Forsythe's advances in movement design and range of interests suggest he is in fact leading the field of modern dance through the vehicle of classically trained dancers working on the forward edge of ballet's inherent possibilities. Critical efforts to define him out of the field and lay down rules for where ballet may properly be headed are made irrelevant by the authority of those who make the work.

KEY WORDS Vaslav Nijinsky, William Forsythe, George Balanchine, ballet, modern dance.

I first heard it from Paul Taylor: the suggestion that the real founder of modern dance was Vaslav Nijinsky. The notion comes, in fact, from Lincoln Kirstein. It rests on an appreciation of the choreographer Nijinsky's profound innovations in movement design and group structure. Perhaps it also reflects that the Russian dancer was committed to a personal vision rather than to the primacy of the classical materials he inherited.

What made us think Nijinsky was a ballet choreographer at all? The answer is probably his context, the Diaghilev company, and his training more than his actual product. Consider the choreographic material of his fully completed works. They could all be taken for radical modern dance, but they were performed by ballet dancers, and presented by a company with an otherwise classical repertory.

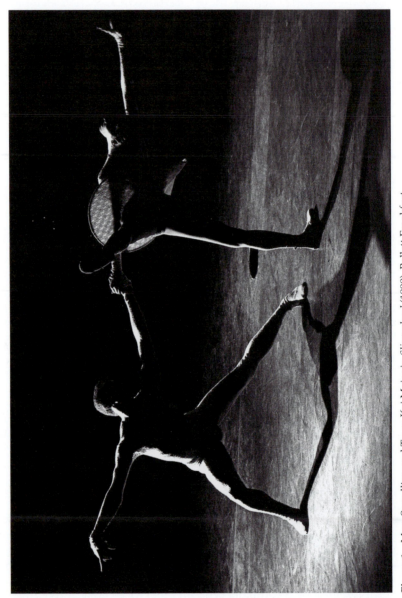

Figure 1 Marc Spradling and Tracy-Kai Maier in *Slingerland* (1990), Ballett Frankfurt
Photo: Marie-Noëlle Robert © 1998

The elements of the Russian ballet tradition were being used to forge an utterly original direction. What made us think George Balanchine ran what was essentially a modern dance company, compared to other ballet companies of his era? One usually cited his departure from the classic repertory and school of steps and his commitment to a single, progressive artistic vision and a distinctive movement vocabulary. Ballet is defined, like all arts, by its makers, and by the dancers and choreographers who accept influences that they find persuasive, and build upon them.

When an artist with a thoroughly classical background is denounced on the grounds that he "destroys ballet", either the work is weak or ballet has developed dangerously reactionary thinking. Those who do not make work are periodically moved to lock down its definitions: this was ineffective in 1912 when Nijinsky created his first full professional work, and it will continue to be so. We can celebrate a profound advance into new thinking when a choreographer spends his artistic life inside the classical school, shows veneration for the *ballet d'école*, informed respect for Balanchine and ballet history, and regular reliance on the pointe shoe, but makes work with unorthodox expansions of the vocabulary, fractured yet theatrically astute structure, and constant sympathies with the work of major modern dance innovators. This issue of *Choreography and Dance* is about one such man.

William Forsythe has given his field a daring new direction and scope. His work is frequently begun in notions about light rather than music, as he reveals in the *Conversation on Lighting* with Jennifer Tipton included in this issue. Like the finest artists, he teaches the dance audience new skills for looking at things. For his sake we have developed a capacity to see in extremely low levels of light, even as his dancers have learned to be able to move freely, in groups, through a blackout. We can follow the logic of a known classical step through long new permutations. A *penché* may plunge in extraordinary directions, or a *fouetté* be created by picking up the dancer and hurling her manually around 360° as she executes the legwork – and we still recognize the source. As Forsythe has often stated, he treats the premises of classical technique as a usable language capable of new meaning, rather than as a collection of phrases and traditionally-linked steps that retain traditional rules, shapes, and content subject only to rearrangement. Aside from his enrichment of the *ballet d'école*, his approach greatly strengthens the dancers who use it. This is apparent physically as well as in their

Figure 2   Evan Jones and William Forsythe, the making of *LDC*, Ballett Frankfurt, 1985
Photo: Charles Tandy © 1998

intellectual development, and it shows up in a look of knowledge-ability and engagement on stage. Most dancers in outside companies who are cast in Forsythe pieces look like different artists in his work. They visibly know what a depth of information lies behind their movement.

Forsythe has taught classical dancers to generate their own material by applying structural devices to their familiar technique. Drawing upon the theories of Rudolf Laban, which Forsythe has carried forward in what he calls Improvisation Technology, he vitally expands the movement vocabulary. His style has developed over the 14 years in Frankfurt from a forceful, weighted, and athletic one using the pointe shoe as a pole vaulter might, into a much warmer and more fluid realm. He has a permanent affection for pointework, and never abandons it for long, but recent works are sometimes danced in socks, soft slippers or even bare feet, and an increasing use of silence and tenderness is apparent. The dancers examine each other, touch and handle and interfere with each other in intricate assignments, and work extensively with and close to the floor. The structure of the pieces can seem confusing, but they are assembled with astute theatricality. They are carefully built to pace the evening well, and they progress with their own logic. His approach and movement thinking resonate with the methods of the great modern dance innovators such as Merce Cunningham, Trisha Brown, and Twyla Tharp. Both his artists and the dancers of other companies who have worked with him demonstrate a range of new virtuosities. These days one rarely sees as much original material for the body in a whole season of modern dance as Forsythe offers at Ballett Frankfurt.

The range of Forsythe's thinking is illustrated by the various plans he made for a new work at the Roundhouse, a former trolley-car turntable shed in London. He has described three successive concepts: transformation of the building into a huge *camera obscura* with the image projected into the cellar onto a field of tightly packed narcissus; video on the skylight atop the building; and, finally, (the actual project) raising the "world's largest bouncy castle", an inflated structure with a trampoline floor in which the audience created all the movement. The piece, *Tight Roaring Circle* (1997), is known to him and Dana Caspersen, who made it with him, as the *John Cage Memorial Choreographic Cube*.

Ballet tells us where ballet is going. Not even the most ardent devotees of what used to be can do that.

We had half expected to see moderns, with their alleged superiority of imagination, take over the classical field. The stream of new choreographers making work on and off pointe for ballet companies suggested to some that the future of ballet lay outside its fold. Are we now looking at the opposite, a classically-based artist who emerges as a profound leader of modern dance? Certainly, in addition to his rich physicality, there is more adventure, more risk-taking in topic and visual design and structure in an evening at Ballett Frankfurt than one finds in most contemporary dance. There is also more aesthetic daring. Many modern dance artists have widened their reach into popular culture and its resources, but no one has managed a surreal parody of a Broadway musical, expertly sung Ethel Merman-style by an entire ballet company, quite on the level of *Isabelle's Dance* (1986). Forsythe is, more simply, a profound leader of all dance, going in directions once reserved for moderns by means of a classical vehicle. He observed in the program of his April 1998 season at Theater Basel, "I use ballet, because I use ballet dancers, and I use the knowledge in their bodies. I think ballet is a very, very good idea that often gets pooh-poohed." He trusts the

Figure 3 Gisela Schneider and William Forsythe, the making of *LDC*, Ballet Frankfurt, 1985
Photo: Charles Tandy © 1998

tradition. He believes it is his, and that it is fertile. What does his work say about the old dichotomy, now that he has opened ballet's physical vocabulary, without losing its classical base, by the use of modern dance gambits?

The following articles cover some dimensions of William Forsythe's work up to this point: the situation he has built for himself, the questions he addresses, the priorities he holds, and the body of work he has created. To be comprehensive about his achievement, including his pursuit of intellectual theory, irreverence, architectural theory, humor, the advantages of computer technology, and the role of children's perspective in the art of adults, requires a book-length treatment. The illuminating factor in his process is his huge curiosity about everything around him, how it works and what happens if something is knocked awry. This and his simple, candid respect for other artists are the elements that stand out.

Forsythe has profoundly enriched our art form in his 22 years of working, taking the utmost care to evade the center of attention. He has a remarkable capacity, such as I have only seen before in the great teacher Helen Alkire, for keeping his mind open and at work on new challenges.

He has forged a new kind of beauty in dancing.

This issue owes a great deal to the advice and help of

| Mechthilde Rühl | Dennis Diamond | Roslyn Sulcas |
| Denise Jefferson | Michael P. Hesse | Stan Pressner |

and especially to Anne Midgette and Dana Caspersen; the generosity of Jennifer Tipton; and the inspired course of William Forsythe.

Choreography and Dance
2000, Vol. 5, Part 3, pp. 9–12
Photocopying permitted by license only

The Life, So Far

Senta Driver

William Forsythe's career is briefly outlined from its beginnings in high school rock-and-roll dancing through his stints in the Joffrey Ballet and Stuttgart Ballet. The first works made in Stuttgart led to a demand for his work as a free-lance choreographer in Europe and the United States in the late 1970's and early 1980's. After his appointment as director, and later Intendant, of Ballett Frankfurt he formed a team of collaborating dancers and artists and created a repertory with which he has won international recognition.

KEY WORDS   William Forsythe, Ballett Frankfurt, Stuttgart Ballet, Rudolf Laban.

William Forsythe was born in 1949 in New York City, and moved to Manhasset, on Long Island, when he was 11. It was there that he encountered two major influences on his life: classical ballet, in the form of a lecture-demonstration unit of the New York City Ballet, and the Black tradition of popular dance and music. He became a recognized expert at the Twist and the Mashed Potato in high school, and choreographed musical comedy productions for the students. In 1967 he entered Jacksonville University in Florida, declaring a double major in drama and humanities, and remembering afterwards that his favourite subjects were mathematics and art history. For two years he pursued these studies while expanding his attention to other activities. He added classes in modern dance at the University with Christa (Himmelbauer) Long, and began to appear in the student modern dance group. At the same time he began to study ballet with Nolan Dingman, who directed a regional company in which Forsythe danced. The first work of his own came in 1969.

Figure 1   William Forsythe, the making of *LDC*, Ballett Frankfurt, 1985
Photo: Charles Tandy © 1998

Forsythe left Jacksonville in 1969 to begin full-time classical training in New York at the Joffrey Ballet School, where his principal
teacher was Jonathan Watts. He was shortly offered a position in
the Joffrey corps. Here he danced in works by Kurt Jooss, Leonide
Massine, and *Olympics* and *Clowns*, both by Gerald Arpino, and
took advantage of student ticket prices to spend every night of the
New York City Ballet's seasons in the State Theater, beginning what
has been his lifelong study of the craftsmanship of George
Balanchine.

He proved a physically responsive student and a quick learner,
and in 1973 he was taken into the Stuttgart Ballet, in the last group
auditioned by Artistic Director John Cranko. Joining the Stuttgart
with him was his then wife, Joffrey soloist Eileen Brady.

A central focus of Cranko's regime at Stuttgart, and one continued
by Marcia Haydée when she succeeded him as Director, was the
development of new choreographers. Forsythe took advantage of
the opportunity to create, in 1976, his first professional work, a duet
entitled *Urlicht* for himself and Eileen Brady. The work remains
today in the Stuttgart repertoire. Its promise was carried forward in

subsequent pieces commissioned by the Stuttgart Ballet, including *Daphne* (1977, with Marcia Haydée and Richard Cragun), *Dream of Galilei* (1978), the controversial *Orpheus* (1979), and his first widely-known success, *Side 2—Love Songs* (1979). Commissions began to flow from other European ballet companies and festivals. By 1980 Forsythe had stopped performing to concentrate on free-lance work in response to the demand (he was to return to dancing in 1995).

From 1980–84 Forsythe made ballets for eight companies in Germany, The Netherlands, Paris, and New York, along with works for arts festivals in Montepulciano and Stuttgart and the solo *Famous Mothers Club* (1980) for Lynn Seymour. Three of these reflected a continuing relationship with the Nederlands Dans Theater, whose director, Jiri Kylian, had been a colleague of Forsythe's at Stuttgart. Another three, including the evening-length version of *Gänge* (1983), were made in Frankfurt, at the invitation of Egon Madsen, then director of the state-run ballet company, and they mark a decisive turn in Forsythe's career. An additional turning point was the period of enforced rest mandated by a knee injury. He spent the time studying the writings of Rudolf Laban, the inventor of a movement notation system and a theory of movement analysis and construction. Laban's proposals became the basis of Forsythe's own method of generating choreographic material.

In 1984 William Forsythe was invited to become director of the company he renamed Ballett Frankfurt. By his own account in a number of interviews, he planned his initial repertory with great care, aiming to introduce his audience to a new direction in dance while taking account of its intellectual and artistic tastes. The existing classical repertory was rapidly phased out. *Artifact* (1984) and *LDC* (1985) presented large-scale scenic constructions and the use of spoken (or shrieked) dialogue along with dance material, and they carried references to complex intellectual propositions. *LDC* was the first collaboration between Forsythe and composer Thom Willems, who remains a key figure on the Ballett Frankfurt team. The next work, *Isabelle's Dance* (1986) was, astonishingly, a full-scale musical comedy, complete with original script and a score sung by the members of the ballet company. Forsythe's signature design of his own lighting began to be a central source of the new work, enhanced by his new access to two stages and a skilled technical crew. Ballett Frankfurt began to tour internationally, with a reputation for advanced choreography, artistic daring, and theatrical force. Forsythe began to teach his dancers to create the movement material themselves, a process which has culminated in his declaring Ballett Frankfurt on occasion a "choreographic collective". The company became a magnet for dancers from every country with a developed ballet tradition, and evolved into a multi-lingual corps, by slight majority American. Nearly every major ballet company in the world requested a new or restaged Forsythe work for its repertoire. Successful applicants included the San Francisco Ballet, the National Ballet of Canada, Pennsylvania Ballet, the Joffrey Ballet, the New York City Ballet, the Royal Ballet, the Paris Opéra Ballet, Aterballetto, and Ballet de Lyon. Amid the pressure of this recognition Forsythe followed a relatively quiet life, by his description, raising two sons and a daughter in Frankfurt and focussing on his work with his own company. He married Tracy-Kai Maier, who had joined Ballett Frankfurt from the San Francisco Ballet, and lost her to cancer in 1994.

In 1989 Forsythe sought and received appointment as Intendant in the State Theater administration, giving him a rank higher than Artistic Director, with additional responsibilities, but also more control over his company. Overtures from France about moving the company permanently to Paris were rechannelled into an invitation to present regular month-long seasons at the Châtelet, an arrangement which endured until the summer of 1998.

Forsythe revised his agreement with the Frankfurt State Theater administration in 1998. He continues to run the ballet company within the State bureaucratic system, and also has charge of an alternative theater in the city, Theater am Turm (TAT), where he is expected to produce work of an even more experimental nature, perhaps on a smaller scale.

In 1995 Forsythe began to dance again, in his own work, first through projects on video and eventually on stage in Paris in 1996. He continues to explore choreographic work for the camera. Further afield, he created, with Dana Caspersen and Joel Ryan, a work called *Tight Roaring Circle* (1997), commissioned by Artangel in London. This was a conceptual work realized in architectural terms and it was "danced" by the audience members, who discovered themselves inside what the creative team called the "world's largest bouncy castle".

William Forsythe has been honored with the German Critics' Prize (1988), a New York Dance and Performance Award or "Bessie" (1988), the Chevalier des Arts et Métiers (1991), the Laurence Olivier Award (1992) and the Denis de Rougemont Prize (1996) among other awards.

Choreography and Dance
2000, Vol. 5, Part 3, pp. 13–23
Photocopying permitted by license only

Forsythe in Frankfurt:
A Documentation in Three Movements

Anne Midgette

Frankfurt's liberal past support of the arts, and specifically of William Forsythe's work at the State Theater, is analysed and contrasted with its current fiscal crisis and the implications for Forsythe's position. The city's cuts and a controversy within the management tempt the choreographer to reduce his company and redirect his work, possibly in an alternative space. His work developed from creative use of restrictions on his budget, and his collaborative method of making work developed in response to restrictions on rehearsal time. The ballets *Limb's Theorem* and *Sleepers Guts* and the video dance *Solo* are discussed in terms of thesis/antithesis and counterpoint form. Forsythe's possible new directions are discussed in terms of their implications for the public's perception of the nature of his work.

KEY WORDS Frankfurt, William Forsythe, arts funding, German reunification, bureaucracy, collaboration.

Frankfurt: An Introduction

Frankfurt is Germany's banking capital. It's also like a stage set: its high skyscrapers occupy only a few blocks, a backdrop for a kind of international activity that seems almost unrelated to the rest of life in this rather small city (pop. 650,000). The people who work in these skyscrapers commute in from comfortable suburbs and villas in the surrounding countryside. The people who live in the city are struggling to make ends meet, in one way or another. For, as few foreigners realize, Frankfurt is broke. Its municipal deficit hit eight billion marks in 1994, and hovers around that mark today.

Of course, Frankfurt used to have money. In the glorious 1980s, it was a veritable boom town. Since Germany's arts live on monies from Germany's government, and Frankfurt's cultural officer for 20 years,

13

Figure 1   *Say Bye Bye* (1980), Nederlands Dans Theater
Photo: Charles Tandy © 1998

Hilmar Hoffman, was a liberal, intelligent lover of the arts, Frankfurt's arts flourished. Newly built, or completely done over, were no fewer than 12 major museums, all open to the public free of charge. The beautiful 19th-century Alte Oper, a ruin since the war, was painstakingly restored and reopened in 1981 as a concert venue. And there were new, more experimental venues: the Theater am Turm (or TAT) and the Mousonturm became known for their small-scale but often cutting-edge presentations of fringe theater, dance, and other types of performance. Even the usually more sedate Städtische Bühnen—the city opera house, theater and ballet, institutions common to nearly every German city—reflected the prevailing climate. Avant-garde productions coursed through the theater; the opera house was led by marvelous conductors from Michael Gielen to Sylvain Cambreling. And from 1984 on, William Forsythe gradually redefined the concept of a city ballet company with Ballett Frankfurt, developing it into an entirely different kind of troupe and leading it to international reknown in the process.

By the end of the decade, Frankfurt was definitely able to compete with Germany's other cultural centers—Hamburg,

Munich, Cologne, Berlin—in terms of its artistic offerings. But then came German reunification. And this hit the cities of the "old German states," the former West Germany, especially hard. The 11 states, obliged to make "solidarity payments" to support the cost of incorporating the "new states" of the East, turned many of their fiscal obligations over to individual cities, placing the latter under a new financial burden.

Frankfurt was in an especially difficult position, because it's not a state capital. Its cultural scene is therefore dependent on city rather than state funding. The cultural institutions of Munich are gener- ously funded by the state of Bavaria; but the state of Hessen saves its funding for its capital, Wiesbaden. This leaves Frankfurt trying to carry a cultural scene comparable to Munich's solely on a munic- ipal budget, a budget, moreover, supported by tax revenues from half as many citizens (Munich's population is 1.2 million). When the crunch hit, it suddenly became clear that Frankfurt was drasti- cally overextended.

The first wave of panic broke in 1993, necessitating desperate measures. Street lights were dimmed after nine p.m. to save on electricity costs. Overnight, the once free municipal museums imposed admissions fees of seven marks [$4] a person. And, of course, the budgets of arts institutions were frozen, and have been gradually pared down ever since. Some institutions have closed; most are struggling. Opera house director Cambreling left in high dudgeon in 1997, berating the Philistinism of the politicians who were tying his hands by cutting his budget. This occasioned a wave of headlines and editorials all over the country, most agreeing with Cambreling's position.

For in Germany, it is an article of faith that the government is morally obliged to support the arts, no matter what. To an American observer, it's startling how much name-calling the Frankfurt politicians have come in for. After all, the city is strug- gling on every level, and is still managing to contribute 8.5% of its total budget to the arts, down from its one-time high of 12%, but still a respectable amount. Even after cuts, the opera house is receiving 54 million marks [$30 million] of subsidies, a significant decrease from its former 69 million marks [$38 million] but still enough, one would think, to make opera. But in a state-subsidized system, arts institutions like opera or ballet are bureaucracies, which makes it incredibly difficult to go about reforming them. The way a company is run, the way its budget is allocated, and the kind of work it has to deliver are clearly specified. Streamlining or rationalization are nearly impossible when all of your employees are government officials, with job security and the right to appeal legally any change to the system. And it's far easier, as an arts administrator, to wring your hands about your dwindling budget and continue to draw your own salary than it is to roll up your shirtsleeves and try to see what can be done in reduced circumstances with the money at hand. This, at least, has been the tendency in most of Germany as budget cuts make themselves felt.

Then there's William Forsythe. Forsythe stands apart in the cultural scene, partly because he doesn't take the situation for granted. He has always worked on a relatively low budget, toured extensively and thus brought in his own considerable revenues, and made no excessive demands. And he is far from accusatory toward the city's political leaders. "The city has been fantastic," he says, "and done all that it could—it's broke."[1]

Nonetheless, the whole system, and Forsythe's position in it, have been major factors in the development of his approach, the whole shaping of his art. And in spite of his "otherness," the financial chaos in the city has made itself felt in the ballet as well. Having recently discovered that profits from his tours were allegedly being channeled back to support other branches of the city theaters, Forsythe is "burned out from this regime here." His response: to redefine or reinvent Ballett Frankfurt, and to take over the management of the decrepit Theater am Turm and reestablish it on the international map as a venue for experimental theater and dance. This is not only a significant move for Forsythe, but possibly a step toward redefining the position of arts institutions in general in the Frankfurt of the future.

Forsythe in Frankfurt

The term "a Forsythe ballet" may have become something of a misnomer, insofar as Ballett Frankfurt's repertory increasingly involves choreographic input from other members of the company. It's not just the intricate improvisations, based on mnemonic devices so arcane as to be wholly impenetrable from the outside—a Tiepolo drawing, for example, in *Hypothetical Stream 2* (1997), "with vectors going out from it," Forsythe says, "like a puzzle, a riddle the dancers have to solve"; or, in *Eidos : Telos* (1995), clocks littering the stage which cue certain responses by the dancers depending on where the clock hands are pointing. It is whole sections of works, like Part II of *Eidos : Telos* or Part III of *Sleepers Guts* (1996) which are actually created by other artists: dancer Dana Caspersen and musician Joel Ryan in the first case, dancer Jacopo Godani in the second. The end of *Sleepers Guts*, certainly, came across—in its first version, at least—as a dialogue in a language different from, albeit related to, that of the first two movements.

Collaboration, the juxtaposition of different voices, is clearly inherently interesting to Forsythe; "I like other people's work." But according to him, one reason it has developed so strongly has been the conditions under which his work has been produced. In the Municipal Theaters of Frankfurt, Bureau number 46 of the city government, the ballet only has a certain amount of rehearsal time. The ballet company is expected to produce a certain number of pieces; it has a certain number of dancers (all, technically speaking, government officials). And this "whole situation," Forsythe says, "has determined how we've worked. Everything we've done there has been a survival tactic."

The biggest issue it was necessary to "survive" was the lack of adequate rehearsal time. "We took 13 days for *Hypothetical Stream 2*," he says. "In Tours, I did a version of it that took six weeks." Rehearsal time is so relatively limited that "basically, I taught everyone how to choreograph. It was easier to teach principles of choreography than to try to work it all out myself. My main step was to devise new methods for creating movement; movement is something that has to form [meaning grow out of his methods]." Ultimately, the collaborative work that is a hallmark of the company is simply "making a virtue out of necessity."

Not that speed has necessarily hurt the work. *Limb's Theorem* (1990), which according to Forsythe was created in 24 days of rehearsal, could hardly have been stated in more eloquent, more compact terms. In it, Forsythe manages to attain a kind of crystalline dance language whereby every movement is profoundly invested with meaning that is untranslatable into any other form of expression than the movement itself. And yet the whole thing unfolds in terms that the word "theorem" might lead you to expect. Opening with a discussion of particles, this "theorem" postulates dancers who are dark, emphatic, in small, isolated groups; Part II moves on to waves, and the point made by more fluid motion is underlined by actual cables which the dancers send undulating, whiplike, across the floor. But all of this ostensibly free movement occurs in the terms set forth by the framer of the theorem, represented by a human figure (a scientist) or the enigmatic man-made construction of Michael Simon's set, which moves ponderously, light as air, a line drawing of metal enclosing an ambiguous rectilineal space and endowing it with a special resonance. Part III, instead of resolving or summing up the elegant formulations of the first two parts, moves the debate out of the realm of pure, clean abstraction into a vaguely unsatisfying world of complex, man-made solutions. The movements are more constricted, more awkward, more laden with the weight of overly deliberate attempt; and the theorem, in the final event, leaves open as many questions as it answers—even as the work preserves a sense of definite resolution. Thesis and antithesis lead not, in most of Forsythe's works, to synthesis, but rather to a broader stating of the entire concept on which the dichotomy was originally based (as if a discussion couched in black and white resulted not, ultimately, in gray, but in a meditation on the entire spectrum of color).

Sleepers Guts also featured a third part that took the work's original thesis-antithesis in a whole new direction, but didn't necessarily answer questions at all. Here, it was the aleatoric element of the improvisational sections that came across, rather than *Limb's Theorem's* neo-classical authority and elegance of statement: deliberately so, but in a way that was less immediately effective. And indeed, the piece was extensively reworked before its next run. The fact that Forsythe often does continue filing away at works in progress is in part another result of time constraints.

"The ideas we're having take a lot of time," Forsythe says, "certainly more than we're given." Especially with his painstaking attention to every element of the show. His extensive lighting and sound rehearsals aren't very compatible with the temporal requirements of producing ballets on schedule for a city house. "He works from the light and the look," says musical collaborator Joel Ryan, who has watched the genesis of a Forsythe work. "That's his obsessive-nervous beginning, where his imagination seems to start."[2]

"I've asked for ten years for the system to change," Forsythe says. "I say, I hope you realize that I'm throwing out several million marks' worth of subsidies. We had 24 days of rehearsal [in which to create] *Limb's Theorem*; 21 days for *The Loss of Small Detail* (1987); 21 days for the triple bill [premiered in January, 1998]. It's so unbelievably wasteful—20 days to produce millions of marks' worth of work. Look, my subsidy is 9.5 million marks [$5.3 million]. If I'm only allowed to choreograph 36 days a year, then it's 340,000 marks [$188,000] a day. Don't you think that's a little expensive?"

All the more so in that Forsythe's production costs are so low. Certainly, he takes advantage of the resources of the theater with the sound and light technicians, but a part of Ballett Frankfurt's budget goes toward supporting technical departments whether or not a given piece actually uses them, thanks to the state theater system. "We have not ever used the painting department," he points out. "We finally said, 'We want to do some painting this year,' but it's all booked out by the Schauspiel [theater company], the opera, so I went elsewhere."

What this means is that the system is set up in such a way that much of the opulent-sounding 9.5 million marks is tied up in fixed operating costs. The ballet, therefore, has kept itself on a strict low-cost regimen, one reason a kind of spareness and austerity comes through in some of the work. "I smelled this coming," says Forsythe of the current financial crisis. "In 1984 I said things are not going to be more opulent in the future." As a result, he tried to keep scaled down. The total production costs for *Artifact* (1984) were

Figure 2   *Artifact* (1984), Ballett Frankfurt
Photo © 1998 by Johan Elbers

5,000 marks [$2,778]; "We sort of kept that as a paradigm. We've been trying to work with as little as possible." Ironically, for a company operating at Ballett Frankfurt's level of international success, there's a struggle for money as well as time. "Any money I wanted to use for art," the costs over and above the fixed operating costs, "I've had to earn myself. I don't understand why we're the only company in the world that has to work this hard."

Forsythe's relation with the Städische Bühnen came to an open rift in January, 1998 when he uncovered financial information that led him to the conclusion that his company had been "used as workhorses to help fill in holes in the budget of the whole house." In any case, the system holds little allure for him at this point, after so many years; his own work is in many ways moving in a direction no municipal theater run on the German government system can hope to follow. His statements about reducing the company's size have reportedly led to some concern, not to say panic, among the dancers; from the present 36, already a reduced number, he speaks of going down to 22, then 16. "You have more time to work, lower costs, more rehearsal time. Most of the pieces now are [for] seven or eight people. It's not timely; 36 people doesn't make sense. To imitate military phalanxes—it's not really what we need to imitate." Furthermore, "we're trying to do less proscenium-oriented work."

For the last half of the 1997/98 season, Forsythe was straining with the limits of dance on the one hand, and Frankfurt's arts institutions on the other. The solution, for the next few years, is that Forsythe will remain director of the unchanged Ballett Frankfurt. What this means is that the TAT may become one of the keys to the company's future: a laboratory in which Forsythe can combine artistic input from both inside and outside of his company, and experiment on a smaller, more intimate scale. The term "Forsythe ballet" may become even less appropriate: it may not be ballet at all. But certainly it will mean a new artistic step for an artist who always seems to be asking what lies beyond what he's been doing, and beyond, even, the limits of dance, in the unknown.

Questions of Context

"Usually the third act I try to keep the shortest, about 18 minutes. I learned that from John Cranko; if I learned anything, that's what I learned from him. It was *Swan Lake*. He cut the last act down to 18 minutes, and it really worked. That stuck in my head."

In his work, Forsythe has continually challenged conventional boundaries: the limits of what can be done in a ballet, the limits of what a dancer can do, the limits imposed by music, costumes, sets.

With *Solo* (1995), Forsythe returned to the stage, reinserting himself into his choreography, but at a remove, through the medium of video, which means that in fact he's not on stage at all. His dance is a counterpoint with the exhalations and tangled utterances of the cello, heaving between his labored breaths. The video was featured in 1997's Whitney Biennial, along with videos by two other artists. The video before *Solo* featured a turtle, moving slowly, ponderously, determinedly through the grass for a very long time. This is video art; a kind of statement, a video aiming at a kind of effect. After it, Forsythe's video, the purpose of which is to document a whole different kind of art, seemed a jarring transition. *Solo's* counterpoint—rapid footwork, deliberate, quasi-geometric movements of arm and hand, all executed with the same sense of a paradoxically broken seamlessness that was conveyed by the bursts

Figure 3   *Isabelle's Dance* (1986), Ballett Frankfurt
Photo: Charles Tandy © 1998

of cello music—and the turtle's lumbering gait were two languages with no point of communication. When thus transformed into "video art", does the dancer's articulate eloquence become a kind of opaque art "happening", framed in the space of a gallery and confronted with a gallery audience's expectations? Museum art has a different temporal hold on its audience than "performance." It is allowed, even expected, to become, in a sense, background; the artist in a gallery is not guaranteed even the limited interaction provided by a captive audience which has paid for tickets and will remain in its seats. At the Whitney, people came, paused, looked, moved on.

But how far is Forsythe's work ever "ballet"? Ballett Frankfurt produces ballets because it is a ballet company. *Isabelle's Dance* (1986) is therefore, strictly speaking, a ballet. Thom Willems produces scores for ballet. As artistic director of TAT, William Forsythe may make other kinds of work as well as ballets. *Isabelle's Dance* may become simply a musical. The spoken element in Forsythe's works may take on a different resonance. His dances might become "theater" rather than "ballet". Forsythe could become what the Germans call a "theater maker" (*Theatermacher*). He might attract a different audience. Newspapers might send theater critics to write about TAT, rather than dance critics; and theater critics will be better able to deal with the work in terms of interaction and dialogue than, perhaps, of movement. Challenging borders raises the question of how far people see what they are expecting to see, or see things only because they are expecting to see them. In a ballet, we think first to evaluate an experience in terms of movement.

1998 saw William Forsythe redefining his context on every level. Not only is his future relationship with Frankfurt in question. The year also marked the end of Ballett Frankfurt's long-standing Paris season at the Châtelet. The theater's new director, Pierre Brossmann, expressed his preference for "real ballets with real music."

Forsythe is seeking a new context in France, negotiating with the Opéra, which would like to see him in the Palais Garnier.

Notes

1. All quotes by William Forsythe taken from a telephone interview in February 1998
2. Telephone interview with Joel Ryan in February 1998

Figure 4 Gisela Schneider in *Gänge* (1985), Ballett Frankfurt
Photo: Charles Tandy © 1998

Figure 1 Dana Caspersen and Thomas McManus in *Of Any If And* (1995), Ballett Frankfurt
Photo © 1998 by Dominik Mentzos

Choreography and Dance
2000, Vol. 5, Part 3, pp. 24–39
Photocopying permitted by license only

It Starts From Any Point: Bill and the Frankfurt Ballet

Dana Caspersen

Caspersen joined Ballett Frankfurt in 1987. She has collaborated extensively with William Forsythe as a dancer, actress, text author, and choreographer, as well as creating her own pieces for the company. She illuminates the dancers' training and the process by which William Forsythe produces work in collaboration with his company. The grounding of Forsythe's method in Rudolf Laban's Space Harmony work is indicated, and its development beyond Laban demonstrated with numerous examples of the operations used by Forsythe and the dancers to generate or modify movement material. Works discussed include *Artifact* (1984), *Of Any If And* (1995), *Loss of Small Detail* (1991), *A L I E /N A(C)TION* (1992), *Eidos : Telos* (1995), and *Sleepers Guts* (1996).

KEY WORDS   Forsythe, choreography, enabling, collaboration, improvisation, operations, Laban.

Questions from Senta Driver; WF refers to William Forsythe.

1. Q: What was your audition like? What do you think WF looks for in potential dancers?

I spent a day in rehearsal with the company. I came during the period when *Impressing the Czar* (1987) was being made, so I joined in with the group, running around creating mini melodramatic scenes involving golden props, and being videotaped trying to draw my ear with my mouth on the back of my head. I also learned a section of *In the Middle, Somewhat Elevated* (1987) and spent some time improvising with Bill [Forsythe] directing me.

Bill speaks of the Frankfurt Ballet as a choreographic ensemble. In many new productions the dancers are involved in several sides of the creative process, so he looks for artists and colleagues, people who are interested in his work, but who also have their own art hearts and minds and don't wait for orders. He looks for people with what I would term dance intelligence: curiosity, fearlessness, and the desire continuously to reapproach dancing. Physically, he looks for the ability to coordinate in highly complex ways, creating folding relational chains of impetus and residual response, using isolation and extreme articulation of head, neck, hips, torso, and limbs. People also need a strong balletic technique, although if someone is extraordinary in other ways that isn't necessarily a deciding factor.

2. *Q: What is the company class like? Do you find the need to supplement it with other training?*

We have a traditional ballet class every day. Quite a bit of the work that we do is classically based and requires that particular strength and the knowledge of those forms and methods of movement connection. We don't have any sort of training for the other work we do except that which takes place in rehearsal. It is an extremely varied and demanding repertoire, and physically it can be difficult continually to be changing styles while maintaining the kind of strength required for each one. Some people go to the gym, some do yoga, Pilates [a training developed by Joseph Pilates], or other techniques. I find the Alexander Technique helps me the most, in that it gives me a method to recognize physical habits, and inhibit the harmful ones so that I can work more simply and use my body more effectively.

3. *Q: In conventional work the choreographer makes up steps, or calls for classical steps in a sequence, and the dancers learn what is shown. Your movement is apparently generated in a different way. Can you describe this? If there are special terms used, whether from company usage or from one of the choreographic theories such as Rudolf Laban's Space Harmony, please use them. In other words, what goes on in the studio when a new piece is being started?*

4. *Q: Does WF demonstrate a great deal of movement material, or how else is it generated?*

5. *Q: How are the sequences put together; who chooses the order of phrases, actions, tasks?*

(To 3, 4, and 5) Part of Bill's beauty and strength is that he lets go of things when they are dying, and he recognizes that which is being born. He consistently seeks to re-imagine himself and the dancers. Accordingly, the process during each creation is different and there is a great range of movement generation modes.

Bill's role in each new piece varies, but almost always he functions as a catalyst and an editor; there are many levels of collaboration between Bill and the company within that framework. I'll give a few examples.

Some pieces are choreographed in a more traditional fashion with Bill creating all the movement and the structure, for example the duet *Of Any If And* (1995). In this piece we worked with video, as we always do. Bill recorded the sessions in which he constructed the basic sequences on camera, with Thomas McManus in the room. It was originally intended to be a danced solo for Thomas in which I would speak, and then later, as the piece became a dance for the two of us, I learned the material from the video and we began to construct the piece. I have found this kind of video analysis to be very informative. Bill's dancing is extremely complex and organic, and the key to understanding how to do his choreography lies in figuring out which points on his body are initiating movement and which are responding to the initiation. This inner response, which we call residual movement, is a refraction like light bouncing between surfaces. In order for it to be effective it cannot be decorative, applied after the fact, but must be the result of skeletal-muscular coordinations reacting to the original movement impulse. Video affords the opportunity to discover how this works.

We used Bill's movement in its original form as phrases, and then it was transformed and splintered. For example, Bill would ask us to collide specific sequences; I would try to do one while Thomas was doing another with his arm under my arm and his right leg between my legs. The resulting movements became duets. In this case, the movement that occurred naturally from Thomas and me dancing together, using Bill's movement, shaped the physical nature of the piece, but Bill directed, very specifically, the whole work.

This kind of material collision was also used in *The Loss of Small Detail* (1991). *Loss* was the first piece in which Bill started working on the idea of "disfocus", of moving away from strong, outwardly directed visual focus and heading toward a trance state. The solo material was produced through Bill either dancing out entire phrases on camera or constructing the material with the dancers. We use this material in its original form as solos and as a basis for improvisations during performance. Additional material—duos, trio and group dances—were developed by applying various operations to the original sequences. "Operations" is a term we use for a large set of procedures that Bill has been developing through the years and that we use constantly in choreographing and improvising. These procedures either modify or generate movement. Bill has made a CD-ROM as a learning tool for new dancers in which he demonstrates about 100 operations, with video clips from rehearsals and performances to refer back to for additional examples.[1]

These operations and all the other procedures that I will be describing are tools for the playful mind, not laws or some kind of choreographic machinery. In fact, we've found dutifulness and the fear of being wrong or of stepping over an imagined line between ballet and other kinds of dancing to be detrimental to our work. The dancer's own curious mind is the most important thing.

In *A L I E /N A(C)TION* Part I (1992), Bill developed the key parameters of the event: the methods of creating movement through iteration (solving an equation, folding the results back into the equation, solving it again, etc.), which are discussed below, and the systems that would determine the physical and temporal structures. Within this framework, the dancers (Christine Bürkle, Noah Gelber, Jacopo Godani, Thierri Guiderdoni, Francesca Harper, Thomas McManus, Helen Pickett, Ana Catalina Roman and myself) developed the movement. We each started by choosing a page from the book *Impressions of Africa* by Raymond Roussel,[2] picking a word or phrase, freely associating away from it to some other word that struck us and then making a short gestural movement phrase based on that word. The source material is only important in that its arbitrary, and often goofy, nature frees your mind to associate and to move among ideas.

We took sheets of transparent paper, drew shapes on them, and cut geometric forms into them which we folded back to create a 3D surface that could reveal surfaces underneath. We layered this on top of the book page, a flattened projection of the Laban cube, and a computer-generated list of times organized into geometric shapes (created by David Kern and Bill). Then we photocopied it. We then drew simple geometric forms onto these copies and repeated the whole process until we had a layered document (Fig. 2). We used this document first to generate movement. Next, we each constructed a list of Laban symbols, times, letters, and numbers from the document, which we used as a map to guide us through the stage space and through the structure of the piece as a whole (Fig. 3). The words that would appear through the cut-out shapes on the document were translated into a 27-part movement alphabet which Bill had created ("alphabet" refers to a series of small gestural movements based on words. In this case H is represented by a

Figure 2   Document used for movement creation and creation of the map, used in the making of *A L I E /N A(CITION)* (1992), Ballett Frankfurt

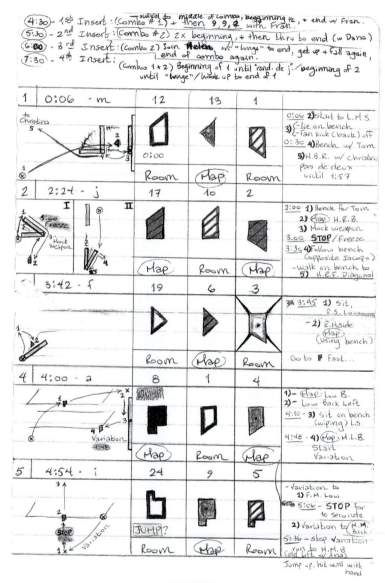

Figure 3 Noah Gelber's map of the temporal and spatial structures, used in the making of *A L I E /N A(C)TION*, Ballett Frankfurt

gesture created by thinking about the word "hat"). The drawn lines connecting the words were seen as a floor plan, and the 3D shapes from the folded paper were imagined as volumes or lines inscribed into the stage space, along which to direct the gestural phrases that we had made.

For example, I took the gesture of my first word: bent arm with the elbow moving high right side to low right side (in the Laban model) and redirected the path of that gesture in space following a shape from the map, which I imagined projected into the stage space. I performed this altered gesture while travelling along a floor pattern, which I chose by picturing one of the lines which bisected the previous form on the map being projected onto the floor. Simultaneously, I began what we call an iterative process. I examined my original gestural phrase and observed where I was and what I was doing when I performed it. Then I re-described that event by applying an operation to it. For example, I tried to draw with my knees the original form and path of my hands in the movement, while avoiding with my ribs the actual position in space where my ribs had been.

I continued expanding on the movement phrases using this algorithm: examining where I was, what I did, re-describing it, and folding the results back into the original material, lengthening the phrases with these inserts and repeating the process several times. Bill worked with us between versions pointing out places that needed expansion, re-direction, more clarity, etc. The basic material that we made in this manner was used intact in solos or as something from which to improvise. I actually ended up throwing out all of my material and improvising on my original word using these choreographic methods.

Using our maps we then navigated the stage. We would alternately read the Laban symbols as directing our limbs in relationship to our body (in its kinesphere), or as directing the placement of our bodies in the stage space; a flattened projection of the Laban cube was taped to the stage floor and low right front was then the particular spot on the floor where that symbol fell. The other information on the map refers to a series of foot stomp patterns which we used to travel from point to point, if we weren't busy with something else.

During the performance there are several kinds of time running: the DAT monitors offstage which show the actual minutes and seconds; a man who reads out the minutes and seconds on stage, sometimes de-synched from real time; the film *Aliens 2*, which is shown to the dancers on monitors facing upstage; and the sound-track of the movie, which was recorded separately and is played at various times throughout the piece.

Our individual maps determined when we had to be somewhere, how long we had to get there, and to some extent what we did along the way. While we were constructing the piece, moving slowly through the structure, each trying to follow the instructions from our own maps, our activities would often be interrupted by something else happening around us. Sometimes the instructions would be impossible to carry out, either time-wise or spatially, in which case we would get someone to assist us in accomplishing the task or we would have to abandon things. All these interactions became part of the final structure.

Once this basic spatial and temporal structure was organized, Bill created a stage environment with a variety of informational sources for the dancers to react to improvisationally. We glance at the video monitors playing the film *Aliens*, and the shapes, veloci-ties, and directions in the screen images are used, or the images are rewritten by "spelling" them with the movement alphabet. A cat [on screen] would be represented by the gestures of the letters C, A, and T. The actual cuts between scenes in the film at some points determine the timing of a particular scene's struc-ture. We "read" each other, the paths of movement, shapes, etc., and we react to the sound track of the movie in a set unison manner, if we hear it. We improvise on our own material using all this directional information. That's how the first nine minutes were composed. Bill constructed the rest of the piece using our movement material and in some cases highly structured improvisation.

In *Eidos : Telos* Part III (1995) Bill began by creating a 130-part movement alphabet. The letter A, for example, is "Abe" and con-tains amplified gestures describing a top hat, clapping, someone leaning over the railing in a theater and someone being shot. He then made four balletic combinations with an emphasis on counter-rotation (movements which have two opposite paths of rotation moving against each other). The dancers collided these combina-tions with Bill's alphabet to produce short, hybrid combinations which he reworked and linked into longer phrases. These phrases were then taken by the company, which separated into smaller groups and produced a series of quartets and octets, using a counterpoint algorithm which Bill developed. The instructions of the algorithm consisted of four directions and four constraints.

The directions were:

1. Effect an *orientation shift* (for example, shift the relationship of your torso to the floor by 90 degrees) moving through plié, while bringing a limb to a hand, and performing an *isometry* (taking the shape or path of a movement and translating it through the body so that it happens in some other area) of an existing piece of the phrase. Take this result and
2. *Drop a curve*, i.e. take any point on the body and, guided by the skeletal-muscular mechanics inherent in the body's position, drop that point to its logical conclusion following a curved path—the desire being to reconfigure the body or to set it in motion in a way that varies from the original sequence. Take this result and
3. Perform *unfolding with inclination extension*: for example, if there is a line between your elbow and hand, extend that line by leaving your forearm where it is in space and manoeuvreing your body to create a straight line between shoulder and hand [this process differs from Laban's idea of unfolding]. Take this result and
4. Perform *internal analysis and extension*: analyze a movement and associate (intuitively find) some relationship between that movement and an alphabet letter. Then do an isometry of that letter. For example, observing the workings of the knee joint could remind one of the mechanics of the gesture for "veil", an alphabet letter, which involves a lifting movement of the right hand. Some aspect of that movement could be reflected through the body to take place in the lower left hand portion of the body, as through a diagonal mirror.

The four constraints were:

1. Find directions, velocities, or shapes in your own movement that link up visually with another person, and align yourself with him or her.
2. Change your orientation, in space and in time (rate of activity).
3. Agree to wait for others.
4. Link up to another by performing an isometry of his or her movement.

The phrases were divided into sections and each person in the group had a different order of phrase components and of algorithm directions to apply to them, for example person #1 had a sequence of components a, b, c and applied directions 1, 2, 3 respectively; person #2 had b, c, a, and applied directions 3, 1, 2. Then the dancers simultaneously performed the resulting phrases, starting at points that coincided in terms of either the letter or the direction. They would observe each other and look for events to which the four constraints could be applied. These initial instructions were repeated and altered as the group worked with Bill to create octets out of quartets, large group dances out of multiple octets, and expanded and condensed versions of the quartets. Bill worked as an outside eye to bring the smaller group dances into a larger structure. He would notice and amplify diverse kinds of alignment which emerged among individuals or groups. The resulting structure has, at times, a complexity that, as Bill said, could not have been created by any one person; the many simple parts having recombined in unforeseeable ways because of innumerable decisions made by the many involved.

Sometimes the choreographic process is much simpler. In *Quintett* (1993) Bill danced the solo material on video and Stephen Galloway, Jacopo Godani, Thomas McManus, Jone San Martin, and I collaborated with him on the duet material, working from our experience of movement analysis and the various operations we've developed. Bill decided the final structure.

In preparing for *Sleepers Guts* (1996), Bill and I had been looking at forests and talking to my brother, John, an ecologist who studies the dynamics of tree species populations based on the competition for resources. We thought about how these competitive processes, with all the incumbent death and failure as well as growth and adaptation, are analogous to what happens during the creative process in a group like ours. The process started with giving out this information. People then had three weeks to do whatever they chose. Bill worked on his own or with whoever happened to come into the room. People made groups and created movement or structures or texts using the forest idea as a basis or not. There was of course, in the end, a lot of highly divergent material and Bill was responsible for the process of editing and structuring the piece. Things that somehow didn't work out in that context, or in general, died, and other things found their way into the piece. There is choreographic material contributed by many members of the company; video work by Nick Haffner and Bill Seaman; text by Bill [Forsythe], Simon Frearson, and myself; and the third act is a duet choreographed by Jacopo Godani and staged by Bill. The structure of the piece was decided entirely by Bill, and the second act was choreographed by him using material from the first three weeks, his own and others'.

The process of editing is difficult for everyone, and becomes increasingly so as the company members take on more and more artistic responsibility. Bill has altered the structure of things to reflect the increasing creative input from the dancers. Dancers are now paid an extra sum for their input, and receive program credit; or when appropriate, pieces are credited simply to the Frankfurt Ballet.

6. Q: *How are the sections of a work put together? Does WF specify all of this?*

In all the works created by Bill with the Frankfurt Ballet, he has been responsible for the structure. There are a few works, created elsewhere and then brought back and re-worked, in which the structure was co-made. In *Firstext* (1995), which was made for the Royal Ballet by Antony Rizzi, Bill, and myself and later brought to Frankfurt, the three of us worked together on the structure of the piece. With *The The* (1995), made by Bill and me, also outside the Frankfurt Ballet, we created the structure together. Later, I took over the piece when we brought it back to Frankfurt, and made the new version, working closely with the dancers: Jone San Martin, Ion Garnika, Christine Bürkle and Stephen Galloway.

7. Q: *Are the pieces and movement set once they reach a desirable form, or is there further indeterminacy built into the form, such as the piece always being changed in some way?*

Most pieces change as they go along, especially in the first few years. Often there will be two or three radically different versions. Then, some pieces have a substantial amount of improvisation in them, so while the basic structure will perhaps stay intact, the content will change.

8. Q: *Talk about the instructions that WF gives during performances to the cast over the intercom. What kinds of changes do you see him making?*

There are a few pieces in which Bill directs the flow of events by talking to the dancers over the microphone. For example in *Artifact* Part III (1984), which is all improvisation, he calls out people waiting on the side and gives drastically varying directions. Sometimes he also gives directions to the speakers: "Woman in the Historical Dress" (which I perform), or the "Man with the Megaphone". In the beginning of *The Questioning of Robert Scott* (1986) the entire company is improvising on stage, based on the phrase we call "tuna", and Bill conducts the currents of events with short, whispered directives primarily having to do with time. In *The Vile Parody of Address* (1988) the dancers are called out at unpredictable times during a loop of music; and in *Sleepers Guts* III, the four women who speak have in-ear headphones and Bill directs us in what to say, based partly on our text from the first act. Misunderstandings occur frequently in these situations. For example, in *Artifact* Part III I've often found myself yelling, "what?!" because it's very loud, and that becomes part of the event. Bill is an extremely curious person and is interested in how set structures change when a few basic instructions are altered.

9. *Q: Are there technical principles the dancers have developed and artic-*
    ulate to each other as part of your understood company style? What
    does the pointe work feel like, and the off-pointe work? How do you
    approach the technique? Are those soft slippers inside socks, as it some-
    times looks from the house?

When I work with new people I find that I end up working most on developing in them authentic residual response, which means allowing the rest of the body to respond in an accurate way, i.e. with physical mechanics that are functional and not extraneous, to the impetus of one point. In the company we work on how to release into these complex coordinations of the body, seeking clarity of articulation without inappropriate muscular control.

Bill dances with great delight. To me, his choreography feels like being a stream, the way water flows over the earth and responds by appearing to take on shapes. Having pointe shoes on for his chore-ography is not so different from being on flat (yes, we do wear soft shoes under socks; it's easier to slide around); the coordinations are basically the same.

10. *Q: Many companies develop nicknames for bits of the repertoire.*
     What, if any, do you use? Do you use French terms for much of the
     movement?

We use French terms if they are remotely applicable, and then we use some nicknames: "Kaiser Strasse", "orange slice", etc. For the most part, however, we need to use very specific language to describe the movement.

11. *Q: When the work is mounted on outside companies, what do you see*
     as technical issues most challenging to these dancers? What kind of
     work (movement, structure, assignment) does WF try with his own
     dancers that is not essayed in outside commissions?

The problem is that there is never enough time for the people to assimilate the style. That said, I notice that the biggest challenges seem to be maintaining the authenticity of movement initiation; maintaining and travelling large forms; understanding the complex internal relationships that inform the movement; and letting the hips drop. We do a lot of work in which the hips initiate movement by dropping and releasing backwards.

When Bill works with other companies he tends to work with their own abilities, i.e. with New York City Ballet he uses a balletic vocabulary. When Bill works in Frankfurt he very often works in a highly collaborative manner: company members choreograph, write text, make videos, make costumes, etc. Bill is an excellent enabler. He has great faith in people and welcomes ideas; it's more difficult to work in this manner away from Frankfurt, with people who aren't accustomed to that type of work and when most of the focus has to be on transmitting information about movement.

12. *Q: How does WF find out about the unusual vocal and linguistic skills in the dancers, skills that he uses in those dramatic turns and interruptions, such as the ranting monologue by Antony Rizzi and the rendition of "Luck Be a Lady" (with Maria Brown) in Eidos : Telos? And your own speaking and writing? Are activities like these assigned to everyone in rehearsal situations?*

We often use spoken text in pieces, and in the creation process Bill will play around trying people out speaking or singing or barking or whatever to see what they're capable of and what they might do naturally. In rehearsals of what eventually became the waltz section of *Eidos* II we worked for several weeks with a number of film scripts and a Beckett television play, virtually all of which finally disappeared. In the end, Bill came up with his own texts, which are a sort of distillation of the work with the film scripts.

Working with Bill people sometimes develop characters and text as a piece progresses. I've created several speaking roles in that way. In the last few years I've started writing texts beforehand and then we work them into the piece or work the piece around them. I've been doing primarily speaking roles over the last four years as I recovered from a foot injury, and writing the text came as a natural outgrowth of this. We needed text for the next piece so I started writing. For *Eidos : Telos* Bill asked me to organize a fugue of text and music. I worked with the composers and musicians, Thom Willems and Joel Ryan, on structuring a small piece that was eventually expanded and developed into the second act. The first section is a monologue that I perform. I wrote the text, Thom and

Figure 4   Dana Caspersen in *A L I E /N A(C)TION*, Ballett Frankfurt, 1993
Photo © 1998 Marie-Noëlle Robert

Joel made the sound environment, and Bill staged it and directs me in it.

13. *Q: What line of connection is there between your own use of WF's processes to generate material, along with all the dancers, and your eventual emergence into a more comprehensive role in building the work?*

Over the years I've developed and pursued interests in writing, choreographing, and acting; sometimes it has worked well and sometimes it didn't work at all. What I've learned from Bill is to direct myself to be equally curious about failure and success, to move continuously back into the work and not try to anticipate the outcome. I, and others who have more comprehensive roles in building the works, move into these positions, I think, partly because we have the abilities to do so, and then because there is an affinity between our thoughts and Bill's.

14. *Q: You may be aware of the sort of assessments of WF's work that are usually published. If so, what is being missed that you see from your experience of the work?*

It would be difficult to respond to all the opinions in general, so I'll just speak of my experience. As I was trying to find a good way to describe Bill's work I came across a quote from the 17th century Japanese Zen master Takasui, who taught: "You must doubt deeply, again and again, asking yourself what the subject of hearing could be." This is the way that Bill works; he doubts with a tenaciously curious delight. He instinctively moves to investigate and explode the layers of ossification that seem to occur naturally in institutions and in the wake of success. I've learned extraordinary things from watching Bill's fearless (or sometimes fearful) curiosity in areas of blindness and sorrow as well as joy, the way that he responds to obstacles and failure as opportunities to re-see. He has a joyous physical genius and an extraordinarily fluid and ungrasping mind in his working, which allows both the sublime and the grotesque to move through him. He trusts himself, but he never assumes that he knows.

Notes

1. More information on this CD-ROM is available on the Frankfurt Ballet website: www.frankfurt-ballett.de
2. Roussel, Raymond (1967), *Impressions of Africa*. Berkeley, California: University of California Press

Choreography and Dance
2000, Vol. 5, Part 3, pp. 41–78
Photocopying permitted by license only

William Forsythe and Jennifer Tipton: A Conversation about Lighting

Senta Driver

On May 19, 1997 William Forsythe and Jennifer Tipton sat down in Frankfurt for an informal conversation about their respective uses of light—and darkness—in dance. They talked of their approaches to lighting design and experimentation, color theory, the design of instruments they now use or wish they had, and artists they respected, manifestly including each other. Forsythe reveals here the central importance of lighting to his work. He lights at the earliest stages of choreographing, making the design almost equal in importance to the movement. Tipton discusses her commitment to artistic self-reinvention and refers to lighting design as "music for the eye".

KEY WORDS   William Forsythe, Jennifer Tipton, lighting design, color temperature.

A signature of William Forsythe's work is its technical dimension: the role played by daring changes of lighting and the action of stage equipment such as exposed instruments, curtains, and cables wired for sound. In lighting design as well as choreography he has led the field. He met the master lighting designer Jennifer Tipton in 1983 when they worked together at the Joffrey Ballet, where he premiered *Square Deal* under their joint design of lighting and slide projections. Since then Tipton has extended her distinguished reputation in lighting dance into theater and, most recently, opera. In May 1997 the artists sat down in Frankfurt, invited to speak informally about lighting and any allied subjects that interested them. They plan to work again together in Austin, Texas in 1999, with Susan Marshall. Marshall

Figure 1   William Forsythe and Jennifer Tipton
19 May 1997, Frankfurt
Photo © 1998 by Senta Driver

has asked Forsythe to collaborate, not with herself on the dance, but with Tipton on its lighting.

TIPTON: How much of the year are you in Frankfurt and how much in other places?

FORSYTHE: We're touring a lot now, because of the money. A tremendous amount, really constantly.

TIPTON: Do you hang on to a certain amount of time for developing work?

FORSYTHE: Ja. It's getting hard now because of the touring, and the demands, and so I'm contemplating just cutting the company down. A lot of people who've been with me for twelve years and longer want to retire now, and it's time. So I'm thinking, okay, why not just scale down? On the other hand, the touring market—the bottom's dropped out. It's like opera: a few high-end places, like Japan or Hong Kong and maybe Paris or Brussels. And London. Festivals have lost all their money.

TIPTON: Yeah.

FORSYTHE: Everywhere. You know that problem. So they're actually hiring smaller, cheaper groups, and I don't blame them. I would too. TAT [Theater am Turm, an alternative performance space in Frankfurt] is really an important link between The Performing Garage [New York, where Tipton works regularly with Elizabeth LeCompte] and the whole world. I would actually rather be in that circuit myself, but we're too big.

TIPTON: Well, it would be wonderful if there *were* a circuit like it, but just for a little bigger company.

FORSYTHE: One's forming, one's forming now. London is also starting to look like a friendlier place, so…America fell out this year.

TIPTON: America has…fallen…out…period.
              But tell me, how do you develop? Do you manage to get light right in the beginning? Or is it superimposed?

FORSYTHE: That's one reason [for the American cancellation]; they asked for a premiere and they wanted to produce it in the theater; and I said, "well, you're going to have to think about this, because I get twenty-five stage rehearsals with light."

DRIVER: *Twenty-five..!*

FORSYTHE: Actually I *can* have it. I don't even use it.

DRIVER: That's extraordinary.

FORSYTHE: Ja. So you develop the work in the light it's going to happen in. But there's a drawback to our system. You probably know that: you've got to be able to set the whole show up in three and a half hours.

TIPTON: Because it's rep.

FORSYTHE: Repertoire. Yes. But even rehearsals for second casts we'll do in the light.

TIPTON: Fabulous.

FORSYTHE: I have fabulous [technical] people here. I'm really happy with my crew here, they're just flawless. And they make such good suggestions. Or they'll change it without telling me [laughs]. I'll be on the intercom going, "It looks *lovely* tonight!" And they're going [innocently], "Really?" [general laughter]

TIPTON: So. How do you reinvent it all the time? I think what I get to do is great, because I go to different companies and different sensibilities, and all of that.

FORSYTHE: Yeah, you do, don't you? And you have people asking for specific things, or you've radically different demands.

TIPTON: Which is wonderful.

FORSYTHE: Well, I guess one of the ways is to make the repertoire extraordinarily different in itself. I make a lot of differences within the repertoire. And I've basically lit one way, which is color temperature [refers to an approach that varies the color of light through bulbs that give yellow or colder, bluer illumination, rather than changing the color of the light with gel]. Single source stuff.

TIPTON: That's a European—

FORSYTHE: "Thang".

TIPTON: —thing; exactly.

FORSYTHE: Although I use color so rarely, 'cause I don't know *how* to use color, basically. But I stick around [gel colors] 201, 202 [laughs].

TIPTON: Right, I know.

FORSYTHE: What I started using was gel as material, putting it on stage. We use it as a sound source in *Eidos : Telos* (1995).

TIPTON: Sound [as] in amplifying it, or..?

FORSYTHE: Ja, ja. We have a lot of complicated digital signal processing music. We made it sound like a giant fighter jet. If you put it through the right things, press the right buttons, it suddenly sounds like the most frightening thing.

TIPTON: Right. And is there a difference between Roscolux [a stiffer form of gel] and Lee? I bet there is—

FORSYTHE: I'm sure there is. Actually you have to use fresh stuff. Because once it gets more wrinkles in it you get too many *small* crinkles. And if you have fresh gel, then it [makes] larger crunches.

DRIVER: But how did it come in [such] huge long rolls,—I mean she [Dana Caspersen in *Eidos : Telos*] gels the light: *she pushes the gel into the funnel of the light.* About fifty yards of it—

FORSYTHE:	Ja, it is a huge piece of it.
DRIVER:	I've never seen gel come like that.
TIPTON:	The movies brought that in, actually. That's where color correction [adjustment of light that is normally yellow with gel so as to make it cooler and bluer in tone] came from, and all of that. It's the demand from film.
FORSYTHE:	I guess I use a lot of film stuff. See, I wanted rehearsal time. I didn't want to spend time lighting all ten sides of a teacup. So I would say, "Let's get it up as quickly as possible so I can work on the dancing." So we ended up just trying to find— there's sort of an arc of plasticity, you know, in terms of height and trying to avoid the front, or anything low from the front, so the picture didn't get flat. And not to make everything look equally dramatic. Well, you know all that. So it's just a question of angle. And color temperature.
DRIVER:	But do you use side positions at all?
FORSYTHE:	Very, very seldom.
DRIVER:	Because you put dancers in the places [usually occupied by side booms].
FORSYTHE:	Well. Sometimes I've stuck an HMI Profile [like a standard Leko but with a very bright blue-white bulb] just on the floor.
TIPTON:	In one place, right.
FORSYTHE:	And seen what it can do. But a lot of that, that lighting…*I don't know how to do it.* How do you do that kind of thing? Like the stuff you did for me for *Square Deal.* Those "*ch-ch-ch*" vibrating things on the side. I don't know how to do that.
TIPTON:	It's so interesting to me, because there are two very different philosophies, I think. There's the American philosophy, and—
FORSYTHE+ TIPTON:	[singing] *the European philosophy!*
TIPTON:	European philosophy is single source, very sensitive to shadow.
FORSYTHE:	Yes.
TIPTON:	And to a single shadow and where the shadow is, and so on. And that's why, when you put a big

source, like an HMI, on the floor, then you're working with shadows, I would think, as much as you're working with light.

FORSYTHE: Yes. And what we would do also is focus it in off [offstage]. We're doing a lot of off focussing.

TIPTON: Well, they are [functioning as] bounce light—reflected light, as well.

FORSYTHE: For example, in *Loss of Small Detail* (1991), everything above the top of the proscenium is hung with a huge cyc—twelve meters high by twelve or eighteen meters wide. And then the top is also hung, so it's a huge white open box, upside down. And then there are HMI's focussed on each of the panels, and on the ceiling also. And—yeah, it's all trying to get rid of shadows. In other words, having had enough single source *with* shadow, I spent years trying to figure out how to get *rid* [laughs] of the shadow.

TIPTON: Exactly. [laughs] Well, the American way, I think, is for the bodies to emanate light.

FORSYTHE: Yes. I try to make a room of light.

TIPTON: It's all about a lot of little sources.

FORSYTHE: Did you do *Antique Epigraphs* [at New York City Ballet, 1984] for Jerry [Robbins]?

TIPTON: Yes.

FORSYTHE: That was *amazing*. Remember? I asked you about that. I said, "Was that *brown*? What *was* that?"

TIPTON: [laughs]

FORSYTHE: [muttering darkly] *Brown light…*

DRIVER: Brown light!?

FORSYTHE: Yeah. Now, you tell me about *brown light*. Is it possible?

TIPTON: [with relish] Of course it's possible.

FORSYTHE: Is it really possible?

TIPTON: You should really take on color. At some point.

FORSYTHE: I'd like to, but I want some instruction.

TIPTON: Who gave you instruction in light?

FORSYTHE: No one. Because I—it was necessity.

TIPTON: Well? Why do you want instruction in color? [laughs] It's much more interesting not to have instruction.

FORSYTHE: Ja, you're right. To use your eye.

TIPTON: Yes, to use your eye, but just take some time, when
             you know that you're going to spend time looking.

FORSYTHE: Actually I think color might be interesting in a piece
             in the rep [*Six Counter Points* (1996)]. I'm trying to
             use this piece of music that Peter Sellars gave me,
             actually. Of all people. He's always giving.

TIPTON: He gave Dana Reitz a piece of music.

FORSYTHE: He gives us all music all the time. He's fabulous. It's
             a gamelan. And I'm thinking that it needs some
             Color. I can't do the usual. But that was an amazing
             room full of light, in *Antique Epigraphs*; that was
             extraordinary. I came out and I was, like, "*Enhhh,
             God, I want this.*" [laughs]. But I was just loath to ask
             how [it was achieved]. I'm watching people's
             shadows, trying to figure where and how you did it.

TIPTON: [laughs] But, you know, color is an amazing thing.
             There is a color, Lee 138, which is this greeny-yellow.

FORSYTHE: Yes?

TIPTON: Try it some time. If you have a bunch of lights and
             you have white light, put that greeny-yellow on full;
             and the white light becomes the *most beautiful pink* I
             have ever seen in my life.

FORSYTHE: What is your white source? Is it tungsten [the stan-
             dard incandescent bulb in stage lights]?

TIPTON: Tungsten, yeah. Same source. Same source. You put
             the color in one, and the other becomes beautiful
             pink.

FORSYTHE: You have them in opposite—same direction?

TIPTON: Anywhere.

FORSYTHE: Anywhere? Any angles?

TIPTON: Anywhere where your eye is seeing them together.

FORSYTHE: And what kind of pink is it?

TIPTON: Unimaginable. Just try it.

FORSYTHE: [laughs]

TIPTON: *You don't believe it*. And there's no other way to get
             it…And the minute you turn off the green, your eye
             gets used to [the remaining light] and sees it white.
             It's all relative.

FORSYTHE: It obviously cancels out.

TIPTON: You see, that's the thing about color, though. It's all
             relative. So white light will look warm when you

	put up the Lee 201/202 kind of thing; and if you put up a lavender it'll look cold. Because that's just the way the eye sees it. It's physiological.
FORSYTHE:	Yeah. Oh, this is encouraging. Because, ja, if I think of it more that way, in terms of mechanics, it seems a lot more appealing. I'm always afraid of the *evocative* properties of light.
TIPTON:	Exactly.
FORSYTHE:	I'm terrified. Because I want people to see things very clearly and simply. That's why I've been sort of loath to fool around. Not knowing how to do it, I don't know how to experiment properly.
DRIVER:	But "experimenting properly" is having twenty-five lighting rehearsals.
TIPTON:	Exactly, that's true.
FORSYTHE:	[laughing] Well, I try to light it in one rehearsal, and then—
TIPTON:	Well, well, and then use the rest for the dance; of course.
FORSYTHE:	And just change levels and stuff like that.
DRIVER:	Or one little gel, that you just accidently throw in.
FORSYTHE:	I lit everything recently with Pané projectors, you know, the big slide projectors [equipped with brighter, cool white bulbs]: just use them without any slides in them. That came out, actually, very beautifully.
TIPTON:	Yes, it adds really a typical German thing.
FORSYTHE:	Ja. Ja. Ja. I've spent a lot of time looking for different color temperatures; using industrial lighting, using anything, just to give different degrees of intensity without using color.
TIPTON:	Do you use louvers? How do you dim?
FORSYTHE:	Ja. Louvers; or I use fluorescents, which is very tricky, because fluorescents are magnificent and horrible; they're very—what is *unberechenbar?*—unpredictable. It's amazing.
TIPTON:	I bet.
FORSYTHE:	Just a little [thing]—a black wall can throw them off. It's very hard. And I find that the angle of the audience is really critical. I've moved around sometimes

	in the house and what looks spectacular in one place—
TIPTON:	[Looks] terrible [in others].
FORSYTHE:	And you *don't see anything.*
TIPTON:	It just looks like worklight.
FORSYTHE:	And I like worklight. I'm always trying to recreate it. [laughs] But they hate me for that too.
TIPTON:	*They* hate you? Who's this that hates you?
FORSYTHE:	My technicians.
TIPTON:	[tone of heavily suggestive scepticism] Oh, *really?*
FORSYTHE:	Every time we turn on the worklight they know I'm going to say—
TIPTON:	[as the crew, anticipating him] "Oh, fantastic! Let's leave it that way!" [laughs]
FORSYTHE:	I do. Every time. Every time. I'm so fucking predictable. I'm trying to be a little less predictable, but you know. I see [worklight] and I go, "Oh why can't it just look like *that?"*
TIPTON:	But isn't that relative too? It's because you've been looking at the other [formal light] that it looks like that.
FORSYTHE:	Absolutely. And then you say, "Okay, just turn on the worklight," and the curtain goes up and you say, "Oh God, it looks *terrible."* [laughs]
TIPTON:	Exactly. Exactly. So you've got to put the cue in—
FORSYTHE:	Yes. Sneak it in.
TIPTON:	And they go, "The dramatic light."
FORSYTHE:	Is it still in? [laughter] Yeah, the worklights snap [on and off], and [so] how're we going to get them out, now?
TIPTON:	Yes. Well, that's the trouble, you know, the question always is: [plaintively] "Can we put the worklights on a dimmer…?" [laughs]
FORSYTHE:	I dare say the worst question in the world. You see it coming. Through the years I've noticed that the difference between too much light and enough light is a very hard thing. Because you want to see little movements at a distance in our profession. You want to see whether the hand is turned *this* way or *that* way. If you overlight it, you get too much reflection,

	and you start losing movement. Direct light has been the most successful way to get detail, I find. It works like daylight.
TIPTON:	Exactly. The room is full of light. And it doesn't come from a particular place. But how much does the light change when you're on tour?
FORSYTHE:	Well, I design it to go on tour. We bring everything ourselves.
TIPTON:	But still, isn't it different in different rooms?
FORSYTHE:	Absolutely. It's an angle thing, too. It's a height thing. The instruments are intended to be twenty-four meters above the stage. But if suddenly you're down to, say, sixteen meters—whoa! You have a big problem, because suddenly the angle is changed drastically. The galleries in this opera house [Frankfurt] are very far out—thirty meters out from the center of the stage. If you're in another house, [for example] the Châtelet [in Paris], suddenly you're twenty meters away; [a] drastic increase in the light. Or in the case of Montreal [Salle Wilfrid Pelletier], [it was] just a disaster because everything was so far out. Couldn't get enough light. We'd ordered a certain number of instruments, you know. What is it—I can't remember—are instruments brighter in America?
TIPTON:	I feel so.
FORSYTHE:	Yes, they are. So we were counting on that, but it [laughs] didn't compensate enough.
DRIVER:	Well, he was in a baseball park. That is the biggest theater I have ever seen.
FORSYTHE:	It is a *hu-u-uge theatah.*
DRIVER:	I know you're famous for wanting big stages, but this was extreme. You could have auto races in there.
TIPTON:	Canada has, I think, messed up their theaters. It's sad.
FORSYTHE:	They're weird. A bit like movie theaters, you know? They're just too wide, and too big. It reminds me of Osaka. In that hotel there's a theater that must have a proscenium [width] of forty meters: there's a hundred and seventy feet.

Figure 2   William Forsythe, the making of *LDC*, Ballett Frankfurt, 1985
Photo: Charles Tandy © 1998

TIPTON: But anyway, so it *does* make a difference. Do you
               take time to make it different in those places?
FORSYTHE: Ja. Absolutely, I have to sit and do everything. Of
               course [you spend] a lot of time, like the obsessive
               fools that we are, going, "take it up a degree, take it
               down a degree." Then all of a sudden it's six months
               later, [you're saying,] "What did I want to do? Why
               doesn't the scene work now? What's [making it
               look] flat?" [indicates that he makes changes during
               performance, via headset, in lighting and choreogra-
               phy]
TIPTON: But that's an opportunity that I don't really have.
               And it makes a difference.
FORSYTHE: Yeah. It does.
TIPTON: People say, "okay, this is the lighting, and this is
               what we'll do forever." But you don't, you can't.
FORSYTHE: I change it during performance all the time. I take it
               up and down, put the wheel on [put a dimmer on

manual control], creep it up, creep it up, till it's working. Especially when we're on tour, because I won't get it done during the setup. So I'll just do it during the show.

TIPTON: I wondered about that. Do you ask for more time than companies generally have?

FORSYTHE: No. I can't. It's a cost thing, so everyone knows I work that way. [My crew is] Incredibly conscientious. I love my lighting and my stage manager. They're *wonderful*. I have this amazing Swiss man, named Urs Frei. He's maybe made two mistakes in thirteen years. I'm not joking. It's really amazing. And I may have changed versions, because the dimmers, for example, for Châtelet are very different from the dimmers for Frankfurt. In Frankfurt we have everything state of the art. So [at the] Châtelet, we know that those dimmers are s-l-o-w, and they correct all the curves for me [adjusting for uneven action of a dimmer across its range]. We do the lighting and then they go in and flatten out all the curves. They'll go in and actually adjust all the dimmers.

TIPTON: Before you're there.

FORSYTHE: Before. They're really good.

TIPTON: That's great. But that takes time too.

FORSYTHE: Yeah, but they plan on that. They also plan for problems. Like in Montreal: there's a big wire in *Eidos : Telos* which is a sound thing. It's screwed into the floor. It makes the whole stage [into] a huge lyre. All the cable had to be specially grounded. We [also] have this huge HMI in the middle of the stage, and it goes right past all the sound wires. And there was something plugged wrong somewhere that was causing this hum, every time the fluorescents in the back on the backdrop were up in conjunction with the HMI. It was a terrible thing. So they spent all night unplugging every stinking thing: every instrument, every plug in the board, every dimmer. They finally found that somebody had reversed *one* plug.

DRIVER: Your crew did this?

FORSYTHE: My crew did that. That's why I say they're fabulous.

TIPTON: Do you ever change the dance because of the light?

FORSYTHE: Well, yes. For example: the light affects how you have to dance the ballet. *In the Middle, Somewhat Elevated* (1988), [has] six HMI's as backlight. It's quite a steep angle, close to ninety [degrees]. And as we all know, HMI leaves trails. On backlighting. So as soon as you start moving your wrists too much it looks very baroque [laughs] and it's absolutely wrong for the style [demonstrates]; you have to be very classical. So I have to constantly tell people, "Look; see my nine hundred fingers? Don't—"

TIPTON: I don't *want* nine hundred fingers.

FORSYTHE: "don't flop your wrists. Be very careful. Because it looks horrible. This is the lighting. So you just have to deal with it." The lighting forces them to be more conscientious, or conscious of it. It's a real thing because you have the cycles in the light. It's slower than tungsten.

TIPTON: I don't know. Might be faster. One or the other. Maybe it is slower, and that's why we see it.
Are your lighting people finding new equipment for you? Or are you the one who...

FORSYTHE: Yes. For example, they're the ones who came up with the indirect projectors the other day. Because I asked them, "Do you think you can make an *indirect spotlight*?" [bemused laughter] And they're like, "Well, we'll think about it."

TIPTON: [as dubious crew] "Yes, *good idea.*"

FORSYTHE: I'm thinking, well, light travels in a straight line: just diffuse light in a straight line. Why not? [laughter]

DRIVER: Is that like the "follow-blackout" that they always used to want us to make? [laughter]

TIPTON: That's right.

DRIVER: "Follow this one around: we don't ever want to see her." [laughter]

FORSYTHE: I've put big mountains of gel, now, on stage, a giant pile of very pale gel, and just lit the stage through a big pile of gel. And that's very, very beautiful. It is gorgeous. Just trying to look at the material itself; because I *like* lights. It's better than scenery. I really don't need scenery for what I'm doing. [laughter]

TIPTON: Light means a lot, I think.

FORSYTHE: It does. Precisely.

DRIVER: Well, you've both demonstrated in your work that lighting *is* choreography.

FORSYTHE: Oh, yeah.

DRIVER: I went up to her [Tipton] at a performance, after the Dana Reitz solo [*Circumstantial Evidence* (1988)] and said, "*You* are the best choreographer of this year." [laughter]

FORSYTHE: Well, it's a counterpoint, obviously. It really is. I mean, everything is juxtaposition. What does Roland Barthes say about the classical? That it's all relational? And it really is. The dance is entirely affected by the light.

TIPTON: Well, the fact of the matter is that light is architectural.

FORSYTHE: Yes.

TIPTON: It's there, in the air, whether you see it there or not. And it makes a huge difference *being* there.

FORSYTHE: It has a presence. What is interesting is to work on building the presence of light, which is why people try to work towards worklight. It's very hard. The closest I got was the other day when we performed in Munich, at the Bacon exhibition. It was just the lighting for the exhibition, which is very beautiful, museum light. It's ambient. But it's hard—"theatrical" is a dubious thing. We all know that. It's very manipulative, and you can make them feel a lot with the way you do that blackout at the end, or the way you bring it up or flash it on. So how do you, very subversively, narrate, without people having felt affected, without—

TIPTON: Feeling manipulated.

FORSYTHE: [laughs] And I like that, you know. I try to do that.

TIPTON: Right.

FORSYTHE: You too? [laughs]

TIPTON: Of course. But that's what it's about. [laughter]

DRIVER: So, in view of that, what did you do to him on *Square Deal*? What was that like?

TIPTON: It's such a total conception. I'm so often facilitating the light of the conceiver, and I'm happy to do that.

[The director or choreographer] should get [associate lighting] credit for it.

DRIVER: How do these places ever let you light something [given union restrictions]?

FORSYTHE: You have to go in with a really really tight concept: really, really, really tight.

TIPTON: Yes, and you light it through the electrician. The way anybody does. That's the way it's done in Europe.

FORSYTHE: Ja. But in America now I just look at their magic sheet [a shorthand plan of the hanging light plot] and I say, "Whaddya got there? Turn it all on."

TIPTON: Yes, what *about* New York City Ballet?

FORSYTHE: I did my own lighting in Canada [for *the second detail* (1991), National Ballet of Canada] but even then, I went with the resident lighting guy to photographic shops and looked at big things, and they copied them and built them. In America usually I try to use what they have. Except in the case of San Francisco, where we did *New Sleep* (1987) [and] I used back HMI's on diagonals cut by the last wing in an X across the stage. A few little exceptional things. But, other than that, I just say, "What do you have?"

TIPTON: It's hard to get HMI's in America.

FORSYTHE: Ja. It's expensive, too. Renting them for six weeks is difficult.

DRIVER: Where do they come from? Are they film?

FORSYTHE: Ja. But I usually like to look at what people have, and then say, "Well, what do *you* think?" I'm more the time person and so they're the *what* and I'm the *when* and *how*. [In] America, the focusses are so *beautiful*, oh. I don't have time to do that. Mark Stanley did the most gorgeous things in New York [over the New York City Ballet] which in no way could I do here. Everything is so clear and beautiful. Because it was conceived, ja? It was conceived in that light.

TIPTON: In that situation.

FORSYTHE: I go in to the designer and I say, "Okay, where are these pipe ends focussed?" And we turn them on, da da di, and I ask where everything is. I didn't know how to do that until San Francisco and they showed me. The light doesn't belong to any one piece. It's just there for the whole repertoire.

TIPTON: That's right.

FORSYTHE: You just use it.

TIPTON: There's no idea of that here. [The lighting is] all specific to each piece.

FORSYTHE: On the other hand, each piece is often determined by the positions of the instruments as they are [hung] in the theater or built in. We have a lot of Profiles in the galleries all built in; they're all in huge armatures. We have virtually all Niedheimer instruments, which are just *wunderbar.*

TIPTON: So, when the theater was built somebody put in a repertory light plot?

FORSYTHE: Right.

TIPTON: For the opera, or for the opera and ballet?

FORSYTHE: They put in the instruments, but you can move all of them. The positions of the big—what they call "Holas" which are the electrical bridges—those are permanent. And that affects a lot. A lot. So, often I have to rebuild a couple of pipes to make an electric bridge. The mind informing the German opera house is obviously part and parcel of what I do.

TIPTON: That's your playground, as it were.

FORSYTHE: Ja. Those angles are given, which is also very frustrating.

TIPTON: Sure. But, they're more or less the same from theater to theater in Germany, too, I would bet. So in touring—

FORSYTHE: In Europe, you don't tend to have a problem. The problem with the [New York] State Theater [was lighting]. We were supposed to go there just now [July 1997]. And I literally could not light the pieces. Because at one [point in] *Enemy in the Figure* (1989) I have a 5K [5000 kilowatts. A large and bright light] on wheels. and it has to reflect off the wall [offstage, in the wings]. There're no walls to reflect off. You'd have to build all this. And even then, half the audience wouldn't have seen it. It would have been a catastrophe. Our prosceniums are so far forward that I

Figure 3   Tracy-Kai Maier in *Limb's Theorem* (1990), incorporating *Enemy in the Figure* (1989). Ballett Frankfurt 1992
Photo © 1998 by Marc Ginot

hang a very reflective gold curtain, 'cause I have tungsten [instruments]. I suddenly turn [a light] and reflect off the curtain, [and the] house gets warm and cozy. This was impossible to do and still have the space to dance. It just didn't work.

TIPTON: Well, the New York State Theater is very small, actually.

FORSYTHE: I'm so glad you said that. Because people said, "What? State Theater [inadequate]?" The producers are angry at me, and I can understand why. I thought, and I said, "Yes yes yes," and my technicians kept saying, "No... no... no." The repertoire I wanted to bring, *I couldn't light*. That was the problem. Dancing and lighting in these pieces are so bound up. *Enemy in the Figure* is literally one light. On wheels. 5KV. The entire piece. So what are you gonna do?

TIPTON: Yes; but it sounds like it's not the light, it's—

FORSYTHE: What happens in it.

TIPTON: —what the one light hits.

FORSYTHE: Well; the entire stage is a lighting instrument, because there's an undulating wall of very pale wood in the middle of the stage and I reflect [light] off it this way, off these big fire walls here which are gray. That color is important. It's a somewhat shiny matte gray, not completely flat. And then if you bounce off the proscenium here at a particular angle—

TIPTON: But, a piece like that you manage to tour [in Europe] fairly easily.

FORSYTHE: Yes. But the proportion of the theater is a very strange thing. [New York] State Theater was built for the wing-and-backdrop show. And the galleries are asymmetrical, for our purposes. I need to light *all* the way out. I can't do that equally on both sides.

DRIVER: What stage is big enough for you? Or what stages will work?

FORSYTHE: Well, the Met is perfect; but everyone looks like ants at work.

DRIVER: Is Brooklyn Academy workable for you?

FORSYTHE: Brooklyn is small, too. Brooklyn is nice, though.

TIPTON: Yes, well, the Met is good because they have those doors that can close. Or open, and have the space—

FORSYTHE: But [there's] the question of selling us at the Met. No one knows who we are, basically. And you're not going to get the subscriptions from the suburbs to come and see the Frankfurt Ballet. State Theater's bad enough.

TIPTON: That's so silly, because it's the same kind of theater.

FORSYTHE: I know. It's basically the same theater twice.

TIPTON: Yes, exactly.

FORSYTHE: However, I do prefer the audience of State Theater. It's a beautiful theater. It's just snazzy. I like ours, too, Frankfurt. Actually that's why I'm there. It's my favourite theater. Ach! it's gorgeous, it really is. A very nice theater also is Reggio Emilia. *Very* generous stage. Beautiful, small little opera house. I always like the proportion when the house is a bit smaller than the stage. That's what we have here. The [Opera House] stage is forty meters by forty meters. The audience is a thousand three hundred.

TIPTON: Great, perfect.

FORSYTHE: Ja, truly. The Schauspiel [Schauspielhaus, second theater at the Frankfurt Opera] is twenty-four meters square; you can completely put the proscenium aside so it's one room with the audience. And it's only seven hundred seats. That's also gorgeous. So we perform in both. My situation here is really a blessing. Truly, truly a blessing.

DRIVER: You've both done a lot of work with low light. You're talking about light: you're not talking about *no* light. Talk about no light.

TIPTON: It's so difficult in opera houses, I find, because there's so *much* ambient light.

FORSYTHE: Well, you have to have a blackout check, like we do. Ja? You have to literally assign someone to go and turn off every stinking thing.

TIPTON: But I'm talking about exit lights, things like that. I get so irritated. I did a piece in Stockholm, and we got permission to have all the lights out for the first two minutes, or something like that—

FORSYTHE: Ja. Ja.

TIPTON: —totally. So we sat—the audience sat [in blackout]. I've never done this before in my life in such a big house. To sit in a totally black house. All those people—it's wonderful. And then...one candle. [laughs]

FORSYTHE: Oh, it's great.

TIPTON: I tried to light a piece with candles. We had seven candles. And I had hoped to do the first ten minutes or something with just candles. It was at Hartford Stage. And I couldn't do it. It was just...too...dark.

FORSYTHE: I tried blowtorches...[laughter]

TIPTON: A little bit different!

FORSYTHE: —and it was so beautiful, because the moving air changed the whole picture. Then it turned out that the house was a national monument, and that blew that. I couldn't have a fire going. But in London [at the Royal Ballet] I did. For *Firstext* (1995) lights snap out. And they had, from *Siegfried*—[talk about] using what's there—a fire wall.

TIPTON: Fire *wall*?

FORSYTHE: Fire wall. It's a little tiny trough, it's maybe five inches high. Eighteen meters wide. And you flip a switch and the whole thing bursts into flame.

TIPTON: Oh, yes, yes, I've seen that.

FORSYTHE: It's *so* beautiful. I put it right behind a gray projection scrim. And the floor was dance linoleum, but for some reason, it reflected. And it was [groans] the *most beautiful thing in the world.*

DRIVER: How high up did the flame go?

FORSYTHE: Oh, couple feet.

TIPTON: It can go very high.

FORSYTHE: Two feet, ja. It was moving. It was flaming. It was so beautiful. And it's *light*. Especially just seeing the flames reflected, because we only kept the drop up this much; or [seeing them] through the projection screen. We tried to repeat it in Frankfurt but they didn't know how to build the damn thing. They said, "No, no, we'll build our own," being very chauvinistic.

TIPTON: Of course.

FORSYTHE: The whole thing twisted. Couldn't handle the heat, and set off all the fire alarms. We had a test, thank

	God. They had to come in with fire extinguishers. I said, "Forget it. Don't even try."
TIPTON:	[laughs] What did you do with this piece, then? Reconceive it?
FORSYTHE:	I reconceived it in Frankfurt. Reconceived it entirely. Just did high sides, you know. Very very clear.
TIPTON:	Does that break your heart?
FORSYTHE:	Absolutely not. But on the other hand [Covent Garden] is *wonderful*. I love the place. Such a beautiful theater.
TIPTON:	It is, and let's hope it will be still as beautiful.
FORSYTHE:	They're only going to deepen the stage a little bit.
TIPTON:	Right. I know.
DRIVER:	Can it accommodate what you are trying to do?
FORSYTHE:	No, we're going to go to the new Sadler's Wells.
TIPTON:	When is that going to be revealed?
FORSYTHE:	Well, it was a hole in the ground when I was just there [April 1997], and it didn't look like they did anything.
TIPTON:	Working with Dana [Reitz] I've become extremely aware of that line between what you look like and what you feel like.
FORSYTHE:	And to be in light is *nothing* like looking at light. Have you ever lit without bodies?
TIPTON:	Not really.
FORSYTHE:	You *can't*, really. You're staring at the floor.
TIPTON:	I've started doing a workshop with actors at Yale about this, and I've learned, for instance, if you're in backlight the audience finds it very distant, because they can't see. Whereas the dancer sees the audience. If there's front light it makes [the onstage situation] very available to the audience; and yet the dancer's totally blinded; can't see the audience.
FORSYTHE:	That's very interesting because most of [my lighting] is above, in the galleries, or hanging above the dancers. And they get used to that, because they can see everything. Except in the case of backlight. Or where it looks very *evocative* to the—
TIPTON:	To the audience.
FORSYTHE:	—to the audience, and the performers are thinking—

Figure 4   The set of *LDC* (1985), Ballett Frankfurt
Photo: Charles Tandy © 1998

TIPTON: "This is like worklight."
FORSYTHE: Yeh. I often have the dancers, if they're injured, go
             out and see a performance; they say "Oh my God, it
             looks so different."
TIPTON: I was wondering if you have them go out on
             purpose. Just to begin to—
FORSYTHE: To see what they're dealing with. The ones that go out
             come back going, "We had no idea it looked like this."
             Of course you can't tell if you're in it; there's no way.
TIPTON: Do you ever see a difference then in their
             performance?
FORSYTHE: Yes. I think people definitely know how they them-
             selves are affected by the entire look of it. *Bob Scott*
             [*Die Befragung des Robert Scott* (1986)] doesn't look
             any different from the outside than from the inside.
             But [in] something like *Eidos*, where there's a juxta-
             position between the projections—clear projections
             of black patterns, high projections in the back, light-

ing with projectors—and then, reflected, some HMI things—it shifts very very radically. It's very dramatic. And the dancers feel—nothing. [laughs] We sat them in the audience and said, "Look at this. Now you know what kind of place you're in."

DRIVER: How did you train them, in something like *Artifact* (1984), to dance full out through blackouts? Especially in large groups?

FORSYTHE: They're so used to doing that. We also have a lot of light tape on the floor.

TIPTON: But when someone comes new to the company is there a training period, or [do they] just have to do it?

FORSYTHE: A lot of North American lighting for dance companies includes shin busters [lights hanging at floor level] and booms, which are also very hard to dance in. Especially if you're doing ballet. So all of a sudden they notice it's a *lot* easier [under his lighting].

TIPTON: They can see the floor. All the time.

FORSYTHE: Yes. They can see the floor, they can judge where they are.

Oh, I've done something recently: I've made shadow projectors.

TIPTON: Really? Fancy—

FORSYTHE: Well, I just put large objects—they can be flat, it doesn't matter what; objects moving around, out of the audience's view.

TIPTON: Moving? So they're on a turntable of some kind?

FORSYTHE: You could [put them] on tracks, [or] on turntables. But instead of turning the light off, simply move the shadow around.

TIPTON: Aha.

FORSYTHE: All those nasty directors were backstage saying, [trills casually] "Hi-" and everyone was staring up like this [laughter], [demonstrates discreet rubbernecking] "Really loved the show!" I say, [drily] "It's on a track, and it's a square, okay?"

TIPTON: I've been looking at it in England [Tipton had arrived from working at Glyndebourne]: the puffy clouds, you know, with the brisk wind? Making shadows on the fields. So you've done something like that.

FORSYTHE: I took four Pané projectors, with four cloud discs in them, and it was *so beautiful*. Put them all at different tempi and in different directions. And—like on a cloudy day, you got these shrinking, expanding things. Now here's one bad problem: it's great if you're doing the Place Theater [London] or DTW [Dance Theater Workshop, New York]; but if you move [the audience] twenty-five meters away—

TIPTON: [Or] you go to Montreal…

FORSYTHE: —you don't have enough light, right. It was so unbelievably beautiful, I thought, "This is *it*. [gravel voice] This is a New Idea." No one's done coagulating and dispersing shadow and light at the same time.

TIPTON: And in space, because that's what you're doing.

FORSYTHE: It was random, too. We actually hooked them up to the sound computers, so they were being made to go faster and slower according to certain sound input. Also we used a lot of mistakes. There's a double-disc projector from Pané, and we put all these texts on it. Just cut up a bunch of text and pasted it onto the [discs]. We started looking at it and it was completely boring and stupid. And as soon as it went out of focus it all got prismatic. It was so beautiful. Someone knocked it out of focus. I was yelling—

TIPTON: Sure. It never would have happened—

FORSYTHE: [shrieks] "What is that!? Don't move it! Don't move it! Tape it. Mark it. Paint it." [laughter] So I'm trying to figure out the *wrong* way to use a lot of stuff. That's, I think, an important thing to do, is to get your *hands on* the instrument. And actually focus, yourself.

TIPTON: So you find out what it does.

FORSYTHE: *Play* with the instrument. That's very important.

TIPTON: And you can do that. They allow you to do that.

FORSYTHE: See, that's the great thing. I don't have that problem here. I can really push the instrument. I can just spend the time, or they'll set it up for me in a room and I can stare at it for an hour and figure out what to do. That's a big advantage.

TIPTON: So how much time in a year do you get to do things like that?

FORSYTHE: Oh, I can do up to five ballets a year. I do one big premiere, which is the big twenty, twenty-five rehearsal thing. But we've been trying to simplify. I recently threw something out. [whispers] The worst lighting in the world.

TIPTON: Well, you see, it's about ideas, isn't it?

FORSYTHE: It was a great idea. The piece looked wonderful. It worked; the choreography was great. [But] somehow nothing came together. [The piece] never had a life of its own. You had to keep resuscitating it; it didn't breathe. They're very anthropomorphic, pieces are. They have to breathe. They really have a life of their own. If they don't, it dies.

DRIVER: Have you ever made pieces that you don't *like*, but that you know are good?

FORSYTHE: You sometimes have to live with a success. I mean, I have demands from the administration [for pieces which] are obviously very successful and work very well for audiences, but we're over it as performers; so we say, "We've done this." And we have the producers saying, "We'd really like that piece from 1987." Oh God. I said, "I appreciate that you like that work, but we just don't do that work any more. I hope you like us still, even though we're not the Frankfurt Ballet from 1987. Or even the Frankfurt Ballet from 1994."

TIPTON: Exactly.

FORSYTHE: It changes so much—people want *Impressing the Czar* (1988) still. And you can't do it. The people aren't there—I had a bunch of *maniacs*, perfect at that time.

TIPTON: It's interesting. That's kind of how I feel about lighting, in these pieces that have been done earlier. Paul Taylor pieces, for instance, that I did way back when. They come back into the repertory: I can't change them. Because I don't know who lit that. I'm not in touch with that.

DRIVER: And you don't have a desire to do it a different way?

TIPTON: No.

FORSYTHE: [urgently] Why?

TIPTON: Exactly. It's not new. It has no juice. It's something that's been done.

DRIVER:	But if San Francisco were doing [*New Sleep*] again— [to WF] do you ever have a desire to relight an old piece that someone else is reviving?
FORSYTHE:	I wouldn't. I don't think it's necessary.
DRIVER:	[To Tipton] It's interesting, because Paul, for instance, will be changing the work continuously, and yet you hold the lighting.
FORSYTHE:	I've been working on *Artifact* for thirteen years. I mean, the ballet's changed.
TIPTON:	That's different. If it stays living, if they're new ideas, then it's a changing thing.
FORSYTHE:	Yeah, I changed the lighting of *Artifact* during the last thirteen years; I've had different instruments. We learned we can do that better.
TIPTON:	Do you ever put stuff in the air?
FORSYTHE:	I don't have to. I've got so much filth in the air [laughter] in Europe. That's a problem in America, but in Europe we seem to have enough crap, from Hoechst, the chemical company down the street. Which is sad. [demonstrates asphyxiation]
TIPTON:	[laughs] Breathing it all the time.
FORSYTHE:	I think if I put something in the air people would kill me. You did [that] for Twyla [Tharp], didn't you, for *The Upper Room* (1986)?
DRIVER:	But you did it first for [Tharp's] *Fait Accompli* (1983). Stolen from yourself—
TIPTON:	Exactly [laughs].
FORSYTHE:	Oh, why not? A good idea is worth stealing. Ja. I'm trying to think now about creating a ceiling.
TIPTON:	I love ceilings.
FORSYTHE:	I love ceilings, ja. Trying to create a ceiling of those big window lights from industrials. I've been looking at lighting from car shoots, ad shoots; and commercial shoots.
DRIVER:	So sometimes the lighting concept *is* one of your initial sources?
FORSYTHE:	Often. Often. Lighting's fun. I'm really glad I get to do [it]. A lot of people don't get to do that.
TIPTON:	No. Well, it isn't that they don't get to; it's that they don't want to.

FORSYTHE: Ja. Ja. I've had to. I have no choice. We can't afford designers here. I get the dancers paid, I have all the room, but the budgets are ridiculous. No normal ballet company in America could run on this budget, I mean the artistic budget. So I have no choice. Sure, [there is] the resident Lighting-Meister and that's it. In the early days in Frankfurt we went on tour with *one* [technical] *person*. I had to focus everything myself.

TIPTON: I'm sure there are many people like you, who have that situation, and who don't use it. Who will let the Lighting-Meister do it.

FORSYTHE: Instead of getting your hands on it—

TIPTON: Exactly.

FORSYTHE: —and finding out, well, what happens if I focus all the lights on the booms just on the floor, and then reflect that into the dance? Or what happens if I light only *one inch* above the floor? Just being bored on tour in Italy one afternoon: "Well, what happens if you do this?" [laughter]

TIPTON: And using your eyes. First of all, asking that question, "What happens if?" And then, getting your answer.

FORSYTHE: It seems to be the big art question. "What if?" If-then. Then you just add the *what*. So in the beginning you have what you don't know.

DRIVER: You're aesthetically open enough in your work to accommodate it. That's not a given in most people's work. Your work is broad enough, your conception is strong and radical enough, that there's room for a lot of *what if*'s.

FORSYTHE: It doesn't feel so radical at all. It feels so *practical*.

DRIVER: You go back to the root of it. You go back to the bottom of it.

TIPTON: All you have to do is ask that question, "What if?" What if you do this? What happens? What comes next? Where do I get to?

FORSYTHE: I'll literally stick another instrument inside of a bigger instrument. I mean, just like wrong stuff, you know; why not? It retains that part of your child-

	hood when you took some Clorox and mixed it with turpentine—
TIPTON:	When you didn't know what you were doing. When you *dared* not to know.
FORSYTHE:	It's very hard, once you get very adept at these things, not to know any more. That's the danger. But I think that that's when you have to start letting go of your own ideas and letting other people have *no idea* for you. I think misunderstanding is not a bad thing. "Oh, I thought you meant—" Or someone hitting a light by accident; you never would have focussed that way. [laughter]
DRIVER:	So all your people are under standing instructions—
FORSYTHE:	To knock things.
DRIVER:	If they hit anything—
FORSYTHE:	Leave it. [laughs]
DRIVER:	Never fix a mistake.
FORSYTHE:	Call someone.
DRIVER:	Take a picture.
TIPTON:	Note it. [laughs]
DRIVER:	Tape it down. [laughter]
FORSYTHE:	And you cannot plan it. But you have to set up the whole atmosphere of the work so that this is precisely what people [will do for you]. People think, "You're such maniacs, it's so chaotic." And that's precisely what it isn't; it is a *method*.
TIPTON:	Right.
DRIVER:	That's what I meant. Your method sets up, and can accommodate, error; as opposed to a mistake Ruining a Precious Concept.
FORSYTHE:	You know, craftsmanship is such a dangerous and wonderful thing. So much of fine art is based on craftsmanship. But craftsmanship is a curious thing because it dominates a lot of dancing. Certainly in relationship to Balanchine rep, for example, which is such extraordinary traditional craftsmanship—he formed a tradition of craftsmanship, or extended it. [I look] at that and think, okay, is everything on purpose? There's so much determinism in mid-twentieth century dancing, you know. We're all

affected by that. In every part, every work, everyone wants to look on purpose.

TIPTON: The question that Santo [Loquasto] and I always ask each other: "Is it polished, or is it slick?" [laughter] And where is that line there?

FORSYTHE: Well, I know "slick" is where we *don't* work.

TIPTON: Exactly. You don't get anywhere.

FORSYTHE: Why? Why? What's the point? If you want to do an industrial, ja. Because you're presenting a product, and you want to look like a living TV advertisement. People associate that kind of slickness with accomplishment...which it is, a form of accomplishment.

TIPTON: Right, well, as you say, craft is a tricky thing; because if you have the craft to do that, then you make it look gorgeous.

FORSYTHE: Yeah, but [it's] craft also to take a very few number of givens and evoke *no* craftsmanship.

TIPTON: Right.

FORSYTHE: I'm always trying to use—it's always a desperate, dismal failure—using bare bulbs.

TIPTON: [laughs]

FORSYTHE: They blind the audience. You can't see anything. You put a bare bulb there and no one can see the work. But you're always thinking, "Well, I want to drag fifty light bulbs across the stage."

TIPTON: They're very beautiful objects.

FORSYTHE: Oh, they are.

TIPTON: But they're also—they're so arty, too, somehow...

FORSYTHE: There's the trick, how do you redefine that which has already been categorized? "Arty". [laughs] I like that. When is it art and when is it "arty"?

TIPTON: Exactly.

FORSYTHE: "Arty" would imply "art-like"; *so "Artig", also "Kunst-artig"*.

DRIVER: "Artoid"?

FORSYTHE: "Artoid"? [laughs] "Art-toad"?

TIPTON: "Art-toad" is artoid.

FORSYTHE: In the artist's garden are art-toads. A lot of lighting is also trying not to be Artistic. Lighting cannot dominate; you're lighting a dance. You've got to make the dance visible or invisible. [About] darkness: I can remember being miserably hammered in America for *Artifact* and for [*Impressing the*] *Czar*. But it was very innocent actually. I noticed over the years working that lighting, given a *little* enough of it, *obscures*. I mean it doesn't only illuminate; after a certain point, it obscures. But [the piece] *is still lit*. And people are infuriated by that. Or the critics are, usually, for some reason or other.

DRIVER: Some of the critics. Some few of the critics.

FORSYTHE: But it is obviously on purpose. I really want the scene to look that way. You want something to be disappearing, or to be obscure. Light does obliterate objects at some point. You can overlight something and have it equally invisible. Put too much light on someone and you really can't see them.

TIPTON: Well, it's what happened with the whole Balanchine repertory, as he got blinder and blinder.

FORSYTHE: Is that right?

TIPTON: Oh, yes. He was essentially blind by the time he died.

FORSYTHE: ...I didn't know.

TIPTON: So the lights got brighter and brighter and brighter. And he could not see.

FORSYTHE: I was wondering about that. I was thinking, God, everything looks so *flat* and bright. Oh, that dear man.

TIPTON: That's why. And it took them a while [after his death] to get back to something that was visible.

FORSYTHE: I wonder about my own eyesight, because I do use less and less obscurity. I tend to want just really clear pictures.

DRIVER: Jenny, you've worked with Dana [Reitz] investigating very low light. Do you see it in terms of an ability to obliterate objects? Or do you see it differently?

TIPTON: I think it's wonderful to be able to be there on the line, you know? The line between what's possible to see and what's not possible to see.

FORSYTHE: And it's a *degree*, or *two* at the most, because at one point things stop. And there's a way that things glow in the dark. It has a lot to do with what you're wearing. In *Artifact*, [one] scene has gotten darker and darker over the years. [It] is just twenty women taking a simple step like this, moving across the stage on pointe, like a flock of birds, sort of evoking the Romantic period. The light is so low, so I can just see their arms moving, really flying in space. It's not about making a dark scene, it's that the scene looks best like that. It's amazing like that. But you turn it up two more degrees and it [only] looks like a bunch of girls, going across stage. That's not the point.

TIPTON: In *Necessary Weather* (1992) we play around with having the ghost-like figure upstage, which is where it's expected. Then we make the upstage figure brighter. Not immediately following, but later, [we make] the upstage figure brighter and the downstage figure be the ghost figure; play around with where in space these figures are.

FORSYTHE: Ja, ja, ja, ah God, there're so many combinations.

DRIVER: It is the most wonderful medium.

FORSYTHE: It really is.

TIPTON: Totally fluid, totally. It's music for the eye, is what I call it.

FORSYTHE: [Cheering] It truly is. Thank you, ma'am.

TIPTON: [laughs] [Forsythe ceremonially strikes her hand] There is as much variety and ability for thematic development.

FORSYTHE: And it's a time medium, too.

TIPTON: A twenty-four hour period.

FORSYTHE: But time is a cycle of availability of light and degrees of light. You have starlight and then you have sunlight. So there're your three basic sources: wood light, oil light, wax light. Then came tungsten, halogen; and now there's some new stuff coming out, industrial stuff. A lot of architecture is demanding the same thing. They all want to work with white light. I'm trying just to get hold of the bulbs now. And the transformers.

TIPTON: And there's sodium. In *Hairy Ape* [Tipton's 1997 production for Lincoln Center] there's sodium.

FORSYTHE: Yellow ones. Yeah.

TIPTON: Sodium. Like the moon is. One of the moons.

Oh, there's nothing more spectacular than a hole in the roof of a theater, and the daylight, and you watch that beam of light as it changes.

FORSYTHE: Well, that's James Turrell's field, ja, I think. We have a Turrell here, at the [Frankfurt] Modern Museum. You walk in, it's a black and dark room. And all of a sudden this amazing purple-mauve thing starts to appear in the air.

TIPTON: Talk about time: I'm sure he takes time, time, time, time.

DRIVER: He *is* time, isn't he?

TIPTON: First Turrell I ever saw was at the Whitney. *Huge* painting on the wall.

FORSYTHE: The square! That cube—remember that cube that was hanging in the air? I must say he had a seminal influence on things, James Turrell, for us all.

TIPTON: Absolutely. Talk about low levels, too. It really reminds you that a lot goes on down there in the lower range. And that to me is a problem with all of these new lights. I so desperately, now, with the new Source Fours [an advanced form of the standard spotlight, giving a brighter, greenish light with greater efficiency], want a reading between .08 and .09, for instance—

FORSYTHE: What is this?

TIPTON: They're called Source Fours in America. They're these new lights, they're 575 watts, and much, much brighter. And they have an even field. The New York State Theater, for instance, has them. They save huge amounts of electricity, but they're much brighter, so [when] you get down low, I want a difference between .08 and .09. I want .085, and .0875.

FORSYTHE: And there is none.

TIPTON: Of course there is none; a number is a number.

FORSYTHE: Yeah. That's a shame.

TIPTON: So the bulbs are all going to be bright, bright, bright. The lower registers are going to get more difficult.

FORSYTHE: What'd they do with the lower register, are they vibrating like that, or—

TIPTON: Well it begins to read brighter, or something.

FORSYTHE: You have to rewrite all the curves and stuff like that?

TIPTON: In a sense, yes. Well, you know, when you're working on borderline things, you put it at .08; [then] you put it at .09 and it seems tremendously brighter.

FORSYTHE: And it is.

TIPTON: And it is. .08 is fine—but .09 isn't.

FORSYTHE: And .08 wasn't quite enough.

TIPTON: Exactly. It's technology.

FORSYTHE: Well, I think someone will come around with some sort of correction device eventually.

DRIVER: Or you'll learn to break it, as you've been doing. You'll learn to use it.

FORSYTHE: I'm sure. Use baffles, or put something in front of it. But at one point you also want to be able to use these things. They should be sensitive. They're instruments. It's like a scalpel. If a scalpel's not sharp, what good is it? The difference between 9 and 8 has to be very fine.

Figure 5 *Dream of Galilei* (1978), Reid Anderson with the Stuttgart Ballet
Photo: Charles Tandy © 1998

TIPTON: And there are probably not that many people who care. But who knows? Maybe they can invent some wonderful reflected-light instruments...

DRIVER: Do you have a wish list, the two of you, of instruments you wish existed? Or things you wished you could do? What would you ask for?

FORSYTHE: Thinking instruments, or instruments that would fly around the room, or something like that.

TIPTON: Point source. *That* would be interesting.

FORSYTHE: Anhhhh, ja, ja.

DRIVER: A point source? What's that?

TIPTON: Well, usually you have a large bulb. You can't make really sharp-edged shadows with it. Because it's—*big*. So if you have a single point that's bright, then you have [a] very dark, single shadow.

FORSYTHE: Ah! thinking, thinking: well: Xenon can do it. But that gives you color intensity.

TIPTON: Right.

FORSYTHE: I would like to get beautiful lines in space that weren't laser, for example. How do you get something really fine, really—one thing everyone tries at some point is to get a very thin wall of light. Ja? Or a corduroy.

DRIVER: Corduroy light?

FORSYTHE: Ja. You know what I mean?

TIPTON: [laughs] Exactly.

FORSYTHE: I would like some kind of [capability of] passing light densities over each other. You should talk in the abstract, you know, just so you can get to something concrete; not ask for something concrete.

DRIVER: Ask for function. Ask for anything. And then [the engineers] should be listening to you.

TIPTON: Yes, exactly. Any of those things that we don't have. In some ways it's about recreating the sun, up close. That's all. [laughter]

FORSYTHE: [laughs] Miniature sun. Ja, ja. Chinks in the wall.

TIPTON: So that you can indeed have a line, you know, a crack and a line of light—with all parallel rays.

FORSYTHE: Or like a strip, something like a piece of tape that would actually shoot out light. That's very fancy of

course; you never know if it would be practical. So
you could bundle all of it—

TIPTON: A bundle of light.

FORSYTHE: My partner Dana Caspersen and I recently tried to
make a giant *camera obscura* for the installation in the
Roundhouse [*Tight Roaring Circle* (1997), London]; and
one of the versions at one point was [using a] hole in
the floor in the center where the turntable was. We
tried to make a *camera obscura* out of that room, so that
the whole thing became like a giant eye, using no lens.
Unfortunately the optics, the physics, or whatever it
was in the room wouldn't allow us to do that. There
was not enough light for the distance. I have one at
home in Frankfurt here, in the bedroom. Because I
don't use the door, there's a hole where the handle
was. And in the morning the facades across the street
are very brilliantly lit. On the wall there's this extraordinary upside-down facade-mural. It's so beautiful.

DRIVER: So if you'd had it, if it had worked at the Roundhouse,
where would we have seen the image?

FORSYTHE: In the cellar. We tried to project it onto a field of narcissus. It was very hard getting that many narcissus.
[laughter]

DRIVER: You got the narcissus and you couldn't get the
image?

FORSYTHE: We wanted them really tightly packed, you know, so
you could see it. Those things were all impractical,
impossible. [But] you might as well just try. See if it
works.

DRIVER: Of course. It's your duty.
You're dancing in the film works [that you're
making] now?

FORSYTHE: Yeah.

DRIVER: It's not exactly a case of returning to the stage; most of
your choreographic work has been done on others.

FORSYTHE: Yeah.

DRIVER: But now you're dancing in your own light. What's
that like?

FORSYTHE: I didn't do all the lighting myself, actually [refers to
the duet *From a Classical Position*, jointly choreo-

graphed and danced with Dana Caspersen and broadcast by London's Channel 4 in December 1997]. I did it with Jess [Hall], who did the *Solo* film [part of the video project *Evidentia* (1996), produced by Sylvie Guillem]. I'm dancing on film because I can be selective. You know, I'm forty-seven years old, and I can pull it off in those takes. I must say the takes that I'm doing are pretty long. But I'm basically demonstrating what I can do. I couldn't do it on stage; but this is how I danced. The dancers dance it this way because I demonstrated this way. When I did *Evidentia*, at forty-five, that was the end of being able to do that. Two years later, I work on a different tack.

DRIVER: And dancing *in* the light? What's that like for you now, after you've been working with it?

FORSYTHE: Well, TV light is TV light. I don't like TV light. It's scary. Unless you have some really great person who's willing to break all the rules.

TIPTON: Which they're not.

FORSYTHE: [whispers] I got one. I got one.

DRIVER: You found a video lighting person who breaks the rules!

TIPTON: [laughs]

FORSYTHE: [whispers] I did. Oh my God. [He's] amazing.

DRIVER: Is it a secret who he is?

FORSYTHE: For now, yes. [laughter]

DRIVER: [resigned] It's all right. Couldn't be better used than by you.

FORSYTHE: What he does is, he louses everything up *in* the camera already. He's very brave.

TIPTON: [laughs]

FORSYTHE: He just ruins cameras, right and left.

TIPTON: That's great.

FORSYTHE: Yeah. He's an amazing man. But you are, in film, really at the mercy of the director of photography. They get all excited with Steadicams, trying moving around. We had to throw out hours of really good takes because we moved into the key light. It's just— awful.

TIPTON: But it's very hard then for you to be *in* it, and then—
FORSYTHE: Well, I should have known better. Now I know that. We would have actually adjusted things ourselves. But we were pretty much in his hands and you know, you get excited by the dancing. It was a good lesson. We ended up with enough material, fortunately. [laughs] But I do like it and I will try to do more. I think the film came out pretty beautifully.
TIPTON: You will do more performing in it, or—directing?
FORSYTHE: I don't know if I can. I've hurt my shoulder so badly that I don't know if I can really do it. Nor do I think I should. There're so many people I've worked with who are still young enough to do extraordinary dancing, and the world does not really see them that much. And I want these dancers to be seen.
TIPTON: Right.
FORSYTHE: Dana Caspersen and I—we dance together, she's my art partner—we learn experientially on a project. We edited the film ourselves, with the aid of a really experienced editor. He said, "You can't do that." "Why not?" [laughs] We realize now why not. [laughter] I must say it's a very fast learning curve in that business because it works or doesn't work and you see why immediately. It's so weird having an *eye you can't see through*. I still don't know that yet.
TIPTON: How to use another eye as your eye?
FORSYTHE: [To] use a device as an eye. To really extend that part of your anatomy into this machine, which is a very different thing. I understand the principle of light now, on film, but not how to compose. And—well, I do, but I haven't done [it].
TIPTON: Well, it's practice.
FORSYTHE: Ja. Expensive. [laughter] Really. It's like golf, you know what I mean? [laughter] Or yachting.
TIPTON: Takes a bit of money. More like yachting I suspect.
DRIVER: Yacht racing. I think. Twelve-meter, America's Cup. Something like that.
FORSYTHE: Obviously it's this huge team thing, so many other eyes. If you don't develop the stock right—there's ways to develop it. I didn't know all this stuff.

DRIVER: He's already got a [stage] team, of great expertise,
              that knows how to forecast the mistakes he'll like.
              Now he wants another team.
FORSYTHE: No no no, I just want to learn how to do it myself.
              [laughs]
TIPTON: Do it all.
FORSYTHE: Well, why not?

Choreography and Dance
2000, Vol. 5, Part 3, pp. 79–85
Photocopying permitted by license only

Sound Ideas: The Music of Ballett Frankfurt

Anne Midgette

William Forsythe states that he uses music in an essentially classical way. His collaboration with Thom Willems and Joel Ryan is considered in this light. Willems has composed almost exclusively for dance and for Ballett Frankfurt for 13 years, working less on specific pieces than on an *"oeuvre."* He and Forsythe share a classical background enhanced by sensitivity to disco and popular style. Willems' music, once chiefly electronic, is moving toward a greater use of live musicians and of improvisation. Joel Ryan, a physics/philosophy student turned musician, has worked since 1995 as a complement to Willems, concentrating on detail and sound while Willems and Forsythe address large-scale structural issues. Ryan is working on computer elements that enable a violinist to produce masses of orchestral sound, and envisions the creation of a bowed mouse.

KEY WORDS   William Forsythe, Thom Willems, Joel Ryan, improvisation, collaboration, counterpoint, new vocabularies.

A William Forsythe ballet is played out within the set of limitations created by a specific vocabulary of movement, light, and sound, limitations over which the choreographer exercises more or less, but always ultimate, control. But it is in the realm of the aural, the musical, that those limitations are most immediately tangible to the audience, insofar as it's easier actually to hear music than it is to see into the elaborate thinking behind the semi-improvisation of a sequence of movements. Furthermore, Forsythe states that "Sound is the most important part of our productions."[1] And it was by drawing in living composers that Forsythe effectively established the basis for what has become the Ballett Frankfurt "workshop", what computer musician Joel Ryan describes as "a school for brilliant people who get to make things together," and the kind of collaborative environment that has since become a hallmark even of his choreography.

From the start of his creative career, the range of Forsythe's musical sources—from Bach to Berg to Aretha Franklin—has reflected the kind of ceaseless inquiry and self-challenge the choreographer brings to every aspect of his art. His selection of music also ultimately reflected an essentially classical approach to the role of music in dance, at least on a theoretical level. In other words, "you get a piece of music and interpret it," Forsythe says; "it's up to you to provide an interesting interpretation. If you have a piece of music, it really, really affects what you do." Certainly Forsythe's idea of "interpreting" a work by, say, Bach is hardly a conventional reading of the music in any immediately obvious terms. Still, his basic attitude toward music's role, paired with the nature of his ongoing artistic exploration, made it virtually inevitable that he would come to seek out living composers, working with a musical language that was able to be as flexible, and to be stated in the same original terms, as his own choreographic one. This *modus operandi* allows him to work within a new set of musical parameters, rather than being necessarily limited to the confines of pre-existing scores or songs.

Mention Ballett Frankfurt and music and most aficionados will produce the name Thom Willems. Indeed, since creating the music for *LDC* in 1985, the Dutch composer has been one of the biggest constants in the Ballett Frankfurt equation, becoming a kind of "house composer" for the company. One way that Willems distinguishes himself in the historic annals of composers who have produced music scores for major ballet companies is that he composes almost exclusively for dance companies, and almost only for Ballett Frankfurt, and is "perfectly happy"[2] in his role of court composer. He and Forsythe are working less on specific pieces than "the development of an *oeuvre*," he says. "There are continually several ideas and projects going on; we look at which ideas are appropriate for which ballet. After so many years, there's no need to talk concepts or pieces. The general ideas are mostly similar; how he approaches choreography is the way I approach music." As far as testing new ground: "All the ideas I can bring up in music," he says, "I can do with Ballett Frankfurt."

A key element in this affinity is probably the fact that both Forsythe and Willems come out of a classical background, and their respective artistic languages are deeply rooted in the idiom of clas-

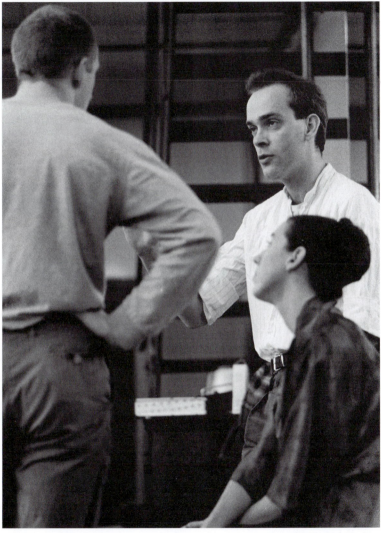

Figure 1   William Forsythe, Thom Willems and Gisela Schneider in rehearsal on *LDC*, Ballett Frankfurt, 1985
Photo: Charles Tandy © 1998

sical tradition. They are also applying these languages in terms of a modern sensibility, with an admixture of modern vocabularies. "I come from a generation that was brought up with classical music and yet hung out in discos," Willems said. "It's very important to have the mix of pop culture and 'art.' The Germans do make a very strong distinction [between the two] but there's no need to at all." The German terms for what in English we call "pop" and "classical" are "U-Musik," *unterhaltungs* or "entertaining" music, and "E-Musik," *ernste* or "serious" music. The non-German sense that both traditions can coexist harmoniously is another point of commonality between Willems and Forsythe (also a member of Willems' "disco generation"). There's nothing incongruous about dancing on pointe to Willems' music, any more than there is in Willems' shifting from unscored electronic tapes to the traditional string quartet of 1998's *small void*.

For the first decade or so of his Ballett Frankfurt work, Willems was producing mainly electronic tapes, one impetus for Forsythe to capitalize on the resources of his technical staff to develop what he now proudly calls "one of the most beautiful sound systems in the world." The incredible precision and high definition of this sound system, in fact, has played a major role in Forsythe's relationship to music in his work. For the sound engineers he works with, who adjust the balances precisely for each individual space in which the company appears, "the system is, in a sense, their work of art; they're used to shaping sound in space. They're incredibly committed. And Thom's electronic stuff is composed to such extremes that it really uses the system." As Forsythe tells it, this kind of detail work has changed his own musical awareness. Forsythe had his own share of musical training, including playing violin and bassoon, but he says that Willems has given him a new kind of "aural training. Thom Willems' music has completely altered my ability to hear music. I enjoy everything much more, hear everything differently."

But in a sense, the Willems/Forsythe collaboration contains within itself the seeds of its own destruction, in that the continual searching for new avenues and learning to hear differently can only bring the artists to a point at which "new" means "without each other." "I've been very cantankerous lately about music," Forsythe admits. "Thom and I are really good buddies; he understands we're both changing."

One way in which Forsythe's work has tested the boundaries of the traditional approach to music in recent years is in incorporating, more and more, live musicians and musical improvisation (such as the instrumental ensemble, including a didgeridoo, in *Sleepers Guts* (1996)). Adding this element is a way of folding the kinds of improvisational systems of Forsythe's choreography, the on-the-edge element of its performance, back into the music that accompanies it; it also emphasizes the human, performative element in the music, as well as in the dance.

"Ultimately, the intelligence of both dance and music is the intelligence of human touch,"[3] says Joel Ryan, who has worked with the company since 1995. "You can do things you can't [verbally] explain, and that's what the art form is about."

Ryan arrived at Ballett Frankfurt to work on *Eidos : Telos* (1995), the second section of which he and Dana Caspersen essentially created. A physics and philosophy scholar-turned-musician, he brings to the Frankfurt table a different array of offerings than the conservatory-trained Willems. "We are complementary to each another," Willems says, and, Ryan adds, "I tend to be the detail person working on sound; he [Willems] can concentrate with Bill on large-scale structural issues."

If Willems is working, in effect, to extend the traditional language of classical music in new directions, Ryan aspires to build new languages with entirely new vocabularies, extending the range of musical possibilities beyond what he is currently able to imagine. Ryan's "computer music" has nothing to do with electronic tapes; rather, he uses the computer to create new "instruments," tailoring a family or vocabulary of sounds to a specific piece (such as *Sleepers Guts*). His creations are therefore less musical "works" in the standard sense than a group of new musical possibilities or parameters within which a performance can be played out. This, of course, makes him an ideal Forsythe collaborator, at least from a theoretical standpoint.

"New music can move forward only as long as you keep making new instruments," he says. "The computer isn't really an instrument; it's a blank sheet of paper. I make acoustical interface so the sound of the instrument proceeds from what's touched"—the "intelligence of human touch" mentioned above, which he feels is so vital to artistic creation. "A violin player can therefore produce an orchestral mass of sounds—but it's all coming from him. The computer acts as a kind of refractor," folding up the sound into many layers, like origami.

The question of live performance—of, in essence, the human element within a piece—is necessarily difficult when computers are involved in the musical process. Filtered through the "refractor" of a computer, the "human touch" is not always immediately apparent in the massed sound emerging from the speakers. Nor is the computer itself a very performance-friendly instrument; Ryan speaks of his own self-consciousness in concert performances at being obliged to "sit there looking at the computer, which I don't want to do on stage," but which is a necessary part of his directing the nature of the sound the instrumentalist is producing. There are possible solutions: "I'm trying to develop a bowed mouse," he notes, "but it's going to take a while."

In essence, this removal mirrors the kind of separation between musicians and music which came about in the 19th century and which Ryan calls "the tragedy of music," whereby musicians became effectively pawns or "workers" in the service of a music that sprung, in the popular view, out of the composer's head. "To a certain extent, in this century, we've lived with a heroic fantasy of what the composer does. It doesn't represent the real collaborative thing that music is. The exciting avant-garde music in this century has come out of ensembles, improvisation." And improvisation, and the challenge of collaboration, are the means through which Ryan's music can flourish in the context of Ballett Frankfurt. The improvisational nature of, for instance, much of *Sleepers Guts* – "We have no idea what the music is going to do," says Forsythe—also echoes the complex improvisations of the movement taking place on stage. Yet the question of the interrelation of these improvisations is complex. In Part II of *Eidos : Telos*, Ryan says, "We're reading our timings from Dana [Caspersen]," but, for the most part, "it's the usual thing of the musicians being in a different world." The improvisations can run on parallel tracks rather than synchronistically. This "separate but equal" coexistence creates its own kind of counterpoint.

Complicating the music-dance relationship, or, rather, lifting it out of the "classical" realm of choreographic interpretation of music, is the fact that Forsythe works seldom take the obvious route of merely keying gestures clearly to sound (the cliché of a dancer's dramatically extending her arms on a *forte* chord). Rather, his movement tends to relate to music by working in a kind of elaborate counterpoint to the score, a counterpoint which takes on incredible intricacy in, say, the last movements of *Eidos : Telos* or *Sleepers Guts*. And informing this counterpoint, more and more, is Forsythe's impatience with the possibilities of relating his movement to music at all. "I used to be in service of the music, providing

an interpretation of the music, but at the moment I'm more interested in working with dance ideas. There's something outdated
about it: get a piece of music and interpret it. We can do it, but we
really don't care."

At issue is the fact that music ultimately establishes its own narrative, which, if it doesn't actually cue it, certainly influences an
audience's perception of the movement happening on stage. Music
"produces the anticipation of having an emotion. What if you just
watch the dance evolve, and have the narration be [the dance's]
evolution? We've been working for five or six years on visual counterpoint—that's music enough for me."

Certainly the triple bill that Ballett Frankfurt premiered in
January 1998, *Hypothetical Stream 2, small void* and Schoenberg's
op. 31, showed the company reverting to a more conventional, neo-
classical mode of how dance interacts or works with music, with
fixed musical works in established forms played to accompany
dance, some of which, such as *small void*, were danced on pointe.
And the music of *op. 31* has "a certain delightful drama," Forsythe
says. "What's there is a structured narrative, very clear counterpoint, and very complicated. You can't be analogous [in dance] to
the structure of *op. 31*; you can only make parts visible." And
there's the inherent drama: "no *Weltschmertz*, but some growling
and then a joy shout. You can hear him going, "Yes!" at the end."

"That kind of neo-classical counterpoint is interesting," Forsythe
says, "to a point. Other structures are perhaps more interesting.
Schoenberg was more interested in twelve-tone." And he's pretty
clear about where his own interests lie. As for his return to a more
conventional way of reading music, he calls the recent triple bill
"the biggest So What? we ever did—a real bomb. People liked it;
that doesn't mean we were satisfied."

All of which indicates that Forsythe's quest for new sounds is
going to take him, in the immediate future, to a new kind of
"musical accompaniment": silence.

Notes

1. All quotes taken from telephone interview with William Forsythe in February
   1998
2. All quotes taken from telephone interviews with Thom Willems in December
   1997 and February 1998
3. All quotes taken from telephone interview with Joel Ryan in February 1998

Figure 1 *Same Old Story* (1987), Kathleen Fitzgerald and Nicholas Champion with Ballett Frankfurt
Photo © 1998 by Johan Elbers

Choreography and Dance
2000, Vol. 5, Part 3, pp. 86–101
Photocopying permitted by license only

Watching from Paris: 1988–1998

Roslyn Sulcas

Sulcas watched the work of William Forsythe during ten years in Paris, and has observed all the repertory created after 1988 and a substantial portion of the earlier works, along with seeing the company in creative rehearsal and travelling with them to Japan. She notes his unusual consistency over the years, that as a choreographer he seems to have been born full-grown. She identifies a number of elements key to the choreography: Forsythe's respect for ballet technique and history, his inclusivity, his personal kinetic imagination, theatrical skill, mastery of form, use of lighting design, repetition, and emotional content presented in a kind of multiple narrative. Works discussed include *The Loss of Small Detail, Artifact, Slingerland, Quintett,* and *Limb's Theorem.* She argues for Forsythe a dual intention: the capacity to make work of great beauty and a resistance to settling only for that.

KEY WORDS   ballet, lighting, theatrical imagination, choreography, multiple narratives.

I first saw a ballet by William Forsythe in 1988, when the San Francisco Ballet brought *New Sleep*, commissioned a year previously, on its tour to Paris. I can still remember my sensation of mixed shock and excitement as shiny black-clad dancers with slashing arms picked their way on pointe along diagonals of light while Thom Willems' music pounded and wailed. It was certainly ballet. Bravura pas de deux and counterpointed ensemble work flashed before my eyes, but in such a radically new context that I could scarcely believe what I was seeing: ballet without quotation marks around the word, as much a part of the contemporary world as film or architecture or quantum physics.

In fact, Forsythe was scarcely unknown at the time. If I had been in France a few years earlier, I might have seen his *France/Dance,* which Rudolf Nureyev had commissioned for the Paris Opéra

Figure 2   *France/Dance* (1983), Narrator Sabine Rothe and Eda Holmes with Ballett Frankfurt, 1988
Photo © 1998 by Johan Elbers

Ballet in 1983. And just one year previously, his *In the Middle, Somewhat Elevated* (1987), to music by Willems, also choreographed for the Paris company, had made of the American-born choreographer a sudden phenomenon—at least in Europe, where he had been working since 1973. But when I saw *New Sleep*, I didn't know that the Paris critics had hailed Forsythe as a "new Balanchine," nor anything else about him. I simply knew that after years of feeling simultaneously bored by, yet still drawn to ballet, I had seen something that made me want to renew my connection to the art.

In many ways, this article is a direct outcome of that first viewing of *New Sleep*, since it was wanting to write about Forsythe's work that led me to a subsequent career as a journalist. Over the decade that has passed since that evening at the Théâtre des Champs-Elysées, I have watched Forsythe's Ballett Frankfurt and his work at every possible opportunity, mostly in Paris, where, serendipitously for me, the company had a "second residence" at the Châtelet theater from 1990 to 1998. I have been lucky enough to see almost everything that he has created during this time, as well as having had the opportunity of talking to him frequently about his work. An overview is nonetheless a daunting prospect. Contrary to some critical opinion, Forsythe's work defies ready categorization. It ranges from neo-classical pieces in a recognizable Balanchinian tradition to wildly theatrical works that incorporate flamboyant mixes of speech, film, video, props, music, dance, and, often, complex technology. All of the work exhibits his genius for lighting. And in addition to the theatrical gifts that are so uniquely his own, Forsythe has extended the vocabulary of dance in a way that goes well beyond the world of ballet, even as he has radically affected the possibilities of that form.

I will touch on a few features of Forsythe's work that appear to me to be central to what he does, rather than provide a chronological overview or discuss a particular aspect in detail. In fact, thinking about how to approach his work made it clear that while there is certainly a choreographic elaboration to be seen over the last ten years, his work shows surprising consistency in many respects: as a choreographer he seems to have been born full-grown, with a distinctive physical style, compositional sense, and theatrical vision at the outset, even if all of these qualities have become ever more articulated as his craft has evolved.

As difficult as it might be to define or describe Forsythe's *oeuvre*, one element nonetheless seems clear to me: that his relationship to ballet is the cornerstone of his work, no matter how far from its precepts he might appear to roam. In earlier works like *Artifact* (1984) or *In the Middle*, the tension between academic forms and those forms pushed to their extremes is explicit. In more recent pieces like *Firstext* (1995), *Sleepers Guts* (1996), *Hypothetical Stream 2* (1997) or *small void* (1998), the slippery, dislocated, densely coordinated movement style may initially appear to have little to do with ballet's formal positions and clear lines, but his dancers' classically trained bodies hold that clarity and articulation within the movement, keeping ballet as a shimmering, elusive physical presence—a reference point to which he constantly returns.

Related to this is a second element that is consistently present in Forsythe's work: a sense of inclusivity. Judging from accounts of his first full-length piece, *Orpheus* (made in 1979 for the Stuttgart Ballet, of which he was then a member), Forsythe seems always to have believed that when making a ballet anything was possible, both technically and conceptually. This is a simple idea, but an enormous one. It means that nothing—whether in another field like

Figure 3   Lisi Grether and Ron Thornhill in *Folia* (1978)
Photo Charles Tandy © 1998

geography or mathematics or mythology, or the history of dance itself—is out of bounds in the creative process and onstage. Antony Rizzi, a dancer and ballet-master with Ballett Frankfurt who has choreographed several works of his own, once put it simply to me: "The most important thing that Billy taught me," he said, "is that anything can go with anything." This is not to do with references or sources of ideas (many of which often appear in company programs, and can engender either delight or hostility because this appears "intellectual") but to do with the way in which Forsythe refuses to keep the domain of ballet away from other domains. It is a point illustrated in a small way by the incongruously unballetic title of Forsythe's *Herman Schmerman* (1992)—a phrase taken from a Steve Martin film—which now seems perfect for the ballet's insouciant divertissement charm because the choreographic universe has expanded to incorporate it.

A third element that is clear in Forsythe's choreography is that the way it looks comes, more obviously than is the case with most choreographers, from his own, very specific kinetic connection to the world. In interviews he has talked about "always dancing" at home, well before he took formal lessons; watching him work, it is clear that he is an instinctively physical person, able to pick up, absorb, and transform movement into a personal idiom, in an uncanny, instinctive, and nearly instantaneous manner. This idiom is fluid, polychromatic, and innately musical, with movement appearing to be generated by the body's own weight and rhythms. Most notably, Forsythe always gives movement marked dimensionality: no step is ever a flat shape in space; it is always a complex volumetric form, existing in its own time.

But what is in fact most notable about the broad configurations of his *oeuvre* is that theatrical imagination always marks the pure-dance pieces, whether in the unspoken rivalries that underpin the heart-thumping, off-balance extensions of *In the Middle*, the friendly, jazzy teamsmanship of *the second detail* (1991), or the heart-wrenching dissolving movement that speaks silently of death in *Quintett* (1993). And choreographic inventiveness always marks the dramatic works: the scrabbling, frantic motions of Part I of *A L I E /N A(C)TION* (1992); the sweeping grace of *Slingerland* (1990); the buckling, shadowy movement that gives corporeal expression to the hallucinatory dream world of *The Loss of Small Detail* (1991). In all of these, Forsythe shows one of the most important aspects of his art: the ability to create a unified theatrical universe, expressed

Figure 4   *Big White Baby Dog* (1986), Kathleen Fitzgerald with Ballett Frankfurt
Photo © 1998 by Johan Elbers

in part by his choreography, but also through an instinctive capacity to edit, structure, and pace a work. (This is very evident when watching him in the process of making a ballet: on a number of occasions, I have witnessed him change a piece entirely by restructuring and often discarding many of its elements, to immediately greater effect. It always seems like magic, which, like all art at its best, is just what it is).

This theatrical ability is most apparent in Forsythe's full-length ballets, where structure, rhythm, and an imaginative world have ample space to reveal themselves. Two of the most interesting evening-length works, *Slingerland* and *Limb's Theorem*, were completed in the same year, 1990, when I first saw them. *Slingerland*, which I only saw a few times during that season, and which is (to my personal regret) no longer in the repertoire, remains for me one of Forsythe's most poetic and magical ballets, with its post-apocalyptic world of scattered stones, its supernatural fairies of the corps de ballet in tutus that look like crisp, curved potato chips, its Beckettian tramps, and passages in which individuals suspended on harnesses achieve the weightless dream of the dancer, yet float (to mysterious music by Gavin Bryars) in vulnerable limbo, unable to dance without gravity. The brilliant *Limb's Theorem*, on the other hand, offers an architectural black and white world in which the dancers are energy-charged atoms in ever-changing configurations of form and matter, bursting into the space like eruptions from the unconscious, infectiously responsive to the light and sound that shape their world.

In both ballets, however, Forsythe demonstrates how ingeniously he is able to shape a work visually and structurally; both ballets are constructed so that different positions in the theater offer different content, and almost no seat allows a full vantage point. In *Limb's Theorem* in particular, the full extent of the off-stage is used. Dancers leaping up against the walls, or a man and woman weaving between long propped-up sticks, and then knocking them over, can only be seen from one side of the auditorium. Both ballets, too, feature architectural forms on stage which frame or shape the dance, and which sometimes seem to change or proliferate as objects may in dreams. (The ability to evoke a dream-like universe in which things have their own bizarre logic and reality is one of Forsythe's most compelling talents). Both ballets are also notable for the way in which they make the lighting, created by Forsythe, as integral to the choreography as are the steps. Exploding and contracting the space, filtering across the stage in uneven and transient shafts, bathing the dancers in a concentrated glare or obscuring them with deepening shadows that intensify the ephemeral beauty of the movement, lighting in Forsythe's hands, in *Limb's Theorem* in particular, is suddenly an explicit, onstage element in the visual composition of the work. (The influence of this on contemporary dance choreographers in France was almost immediately perceptible; it is still odd to me not to see it in the U.S., even if it can be a relief to be spared the more excessive reflections of Forsythe's work that are sometimes, wrongly, represented as "Forsythian" style.)

All of these elements: theatrical imagination, formal mastery, and lighting as a structural presence, are visible in one of the first ballets that Forsythe made for Ballett Frankfurt after taking up the position of director in 1984. *Artifact*, which is still in the company's repertoire, in many ways remains a paradigmatic work. Forsythe showed that he was not simply working with ballet technique in innovative ways, but was also intensely aware of its history as an art form and its potential to go beyond that history. A four-part, full-evening work to piano music by Eva Crossman-Hecht,

Figure 5   Desmond Richardson and Francesca Harper in *The Vertiginous Thrill of Exactitude* (1996), Ballett Frankfurt
Photo © 1998 by Dominik Mentzos

J.S. Bach, and a sound collage by Forsythe himself, the ballet is cen-
tered around three characters: "Woman in Historical Costume,"
"Person with Megaphone," and a ghostly all-over grey "Other
Person," who move like figures from dreams amidst a large corps
de ballet of beautifully symmetrical lines and formations. Using a
limited range of word choices (I/You, He/She/They; Always/Never,
Remember/Forget; See, Hear, Think, Say, Do; Rocks, Dirt, Sand,
Soot, Dust), the woman creates apparently endless narratives, starting and stopping the music and the dance by clapping her hands
like a répétiteur, while the man with the megaphone and the
"ghost" attempt to communicate by means of different hand and
arm signals that are copied by the other dancers at various points.
Repetitive ensemble sequences such as variations upon *tendu* with
épaulement, a recurring motif in Forsythe's work to this day, and the
arbitrariness and restrictiveness of the text seem analogous to the
combinations of steps performed by the dancers.

Sweeping through an extraordinary range of group and individual formations while the lighting renders the dancers successively
present and unreal, *Artifact* sometimes seems like a huge dance
processor, chopping up and spitting out bits of Petipa ("More impe-
rial," I once heard Forsythe tell the female dancers in rehearsal as
they moved in a paired courtly procession down to the front of the
stage) and Balanchine, Laban and Bausch. But the ballet is uniquely
Forsythian in demonstrating everything that dance had thought it
could do in its short theatrical life, and then more. In the pure-
dance, second part of the work, to Bach's *Chaconne* from the *Partita
No. 1 for solo violin in D minor*, two couples surge unexpectedly from
the lines of dancers at the sides and back of the stage, performing
simultaneous pas de deux of breathtaking beauty which are bru-
tally interrupted several times by the curtain crashing down (and,
lined with wooden battens, it really does crash).

It's easy to see this strategy as pure provocation—when you first
see the work, it is nerve-wracking (Has something gone wrong? Is
someone hurt? What is the audience supposed to do?) But the unin-
terrupted flow of the gorgeous, melancholy violin, and the renewed
vision, flooded with golden light, that the ballet offers each time the
curtain goes back up to reveal the dancers, still moving through
another exquisite formation, takes Forsythe's device well beyond
the realm of the sensational. And although *Artifact* makes central
the way dance works on stage in relation to the other components
of theatrical experience and illusion (lighting, framing, the handling

of expectations), it has never seemed to me that the ballet is "about" this in a purely intellectual way. What Part II of the ballet does do, however, is to provide an early and perfect illustration of a duality that Forsythe juggles with through much of his work: the desire for and capacity to attain beauty, and the resistance to settling for beauty.

This tension is also central to another Forsythe ballet that remains emblematic in his repertoire, the hour-long, complex *Die Befragung des Robert Scott* (1986), made two years after *Artifact*. The ambiguities and impossibilities of perfection, or completion, the seeds of dissolution in the dancing body, are contained in a series of solos based on improvisational techniques that Forsythe had been working on with the company. In *Robert Scott*, the movement takes on a new, particularized quality as the dancers focus on making detailed connections between body parts, their ballet-trained limbs stretching and extending in familiar fashion, then mutating into complex, hard-to-read configurations. Perhaps for the first time Forsythe saw that he could actually develop a physical "language" of his own. The working idea for *Robert Scott*, he later said, was "losing your point of orientation," and he did this well enough also to find a new one. The physical explorations in *Robert Scott* that had dancers using their bodies in a newly conceived way to create movement set Forsythe (and his dancers) on a choreographic path that he and they had already begun to explore in other ways. They began spending rehearsal time not just making steps, but also talking, drawing, bringing their lives into the dance; not unusual techniques for many contemporary dance companies, but unheard-of for a ballet troupe. What is already visible in *Artifact*—that movement could be question rather than answer, even as it momentarily answers to a longing for perfection—is explicitly articulated in *Robert Scott*.

Robert Scott, followed by *The Vile Parody of Address* (1988), then *Slingerland* and *Limb's Theorem*, offered the Frankfurt dancers chances to explore the liquid, seamless geometries of movement that they could make by applying new techniques that Forsythe was developing in the course of making these pieces, while continuing to choreograph more balletic pieces like *In the Middle, New Sleep*, and *Behind the China Dogs* (1988) for other companies. The most important of these techniques was "reading externally," which Forsythe describes as "using your perception, your sight, or sense of touch, to read events … you could look at your fingerprints, or a three-dimensional object, and understand how it functioned as a two-dimensional plan. Then you physically retranslate it back into a three-dimensional event."[1] But while the details of these techniques are interesting, it is the results and effects they produce that are most important.

Whether or not one knows how the movement was made, the opening moments of *Limb's Theorem* are magical—movement born from nothing and then endlessly elaborated in ever-changing variations on themes. The dancers' bodies appear as polyphonous instruments that can generate movement from any point, rather than taking impetus primarily from the legs or arms around a vertical trunk. A motif of "arrangement" pervades the dancing: an opening pas de deux has the dancers pulling one another's bodies into balletic shapes, legs stiff and straight, arms held correctly in classical positions, but ignoring the conventional logic that governs the planes and impulses of steps. Any part of the body appears able to determine momentum and direction in an angled, disjointed, slightly scary solo for the central "Enemy" figure in Part II as he makes his way down the diagonal, limbs locking and snapping into position, hands clasping elbows, his white-clad body inscribing convulsive geometrical figures in the air as if caught in a succession of freeze frames. In parallel fashion, the dancing, a constant proliferation and dispersal of pas de deux, solos, trios and group ensembles, is decentralized and unpredictably generated; combinations of these forms often taking place simultaneously without any perceptible relation to one other.

Repetition dominates *Limb's Theorem*: the ball that keeps reiterating its rolling trajectory like an uneasy reminder of something just beyond the reach of memory; the lights that keep masking and revealing the dancers' fugitive motions; the large objects that carve and populate the stage; the recurrent leap against the wall; the frozen moments; the music ticking as time seems to expand into space. At the same time, the work is profligate, exuberant, bewildering in its inventiveness. This pairing, repetition and proliferation, is another element fundamental to all of Forsythe's works, even the focused ballets that he has made for other companies. The proliferation also extends, in the larger-scale works, to props, which tend to be few, but to reappear in different contexts and serve different purposes with remarkable economy of means.

Repetition and proliferation are key elements both dramatically and choreographically in the beautiful 1991 *The Loss of Small*

Detail,[2] which uses *the second detail* as an opening section, contrasting its balletic, counterpointed, rhythmic choreography with the boneless, dissolving movement that characterizes Part II. In this section, Forsythe evokes a physical transparency, with movement that seems to have given up all notions of strength to find another kind of internal momentum. Ballet is visible within its shapes, but not dominant, as if the dynamics that generate it have been removed, leaving traces upon the body. For the first time, this way of moving is sustained throughout a whole work, the dance constantly engendered through internal coordinations (a connection between hip and hand, for example) rather than steps as such, creating an impression of a seamless, prodigious proliferation of motion. And the cheerful rehearsal-room atmosphere of *the second detail* makes way for a blanched universe of myth and symbol, poem and nightmare. Like members of a tribe, the dancers are surrounded by their artifacts, subsumed by forces over which they have no control (Dana Caspersen lifted in slow motion, again and again, away from the table where she is desperately trying to write a message, papers flying into the air; pulled away repeatedly by the same man as she tries to whisper into a microphone; a man desperately shoveling snow into the air as it continues to fall steadily.)

This same kind of physical "transparency," in which movement seems to be tracing an inner muscular process as it passes through the body, can be seen in *As a Garden in this Setting* (1992), made a year later. Even more pointedly than in *Loss of Small Detail*, the movement here tends towards dissolution and disintegration, as the dancers, clothed in bright silk bits and pieces by Issey Miyake move singly or in small groups to a muted score by Willems filled with bucolic noises of insects, birds, and children's voices. Repetitive, sloping, heel-kicking walks by lone dancers form a rhythmic background to long solos and duos in which the dancers' limbs seem to be trembling and buckling at the edges of frailty. In *As a Garden*, Forsythe appeared to be attempting to let go entirely of controlled movement while retaining an internal form that comes from the dancers' highly detailed renditions. That he was concerned with this in the same year as he made *Herman Schmerman*, a witty exegesis on crisp New York City Ballet style and technique, may seem odd at first, but a close look at *Herman*, or any of the "ballet" ballets, shows the same attention to form and dynamics, simply in a different idiom.

Figure 6   *Time Cycle* (1979), Nora Kimball with the Stuttgart Ballet
Photo: Charles Tandy © 1998

The choreographic developments of the kind to be seen in *Loss* or
As a Garden have brought with them their own emotive overtones.
The sight of the dancers disarmed of balletic certitude, moving
without the physical orientation that we are accustomed to seeing
on stage, can evoke a mixture of fear and tenderness, admiration
and curiosity. Perhaps the most explicit articulation of this state
and the technique that Forsythe calls "disfocus" is probably to be
found in the 1993 *Quintett*, in which the dance seems the physical
embodiment of a stripped, purified theatrical universe at once terri-
fying in its nakedness and intensely beautiful because of it.
Quintett's dancers are like *King Lear's* "bare, forked man," vulnerable creatures moving with unsteady, uncertain movements that dis-
solve into and collapse upon each other. As Gavin Bryars's
haunting music, *Jesus's Blood Never Failed Me Yet*, gradually becomes
audible as a quavering repetition of the titular refrain, they appear
to acquire strength in seamless, bewilderingly poignant solos, duos,
and ensembles, in which the interwoven partnering, the kinetic
reactions, the falling, swooping, skimming movements look so
spontaneous that it is hard to conceive of this as "choreography".

At the end, a woman stands in the beam of the light-machine/rocket-object on one side of the stage, then drifts backward to fall into an open trap-door, only to be caught and propelled out again as the curtain descends. A moving testament to the need to endure, to resist anomie, to create, *Quintett* is deeply emotional in a way that characterizes few Forsythe works. But emotion is nonetheless present in all of Forsythe's work, sometimes overwhelmingly so. This is the last element which I would insist upon as fundamental. The emotion is, however, engendered by a complex mix of movement and context, rather than as a specific or desired "mood". Forsythe's lack of linear narrativity combined with his prodigious imagination is often the source of an onstage emotional chaos that can be harrowing because the connections between events feel perceptible yet just beyond conscious grasp. He likes to introduce new elements, obliging the spectator to look again, think again, feel again. The curtains that crash down in *Artifact*, the man who spews forth invective amidst the gorgeous waltz in Part 2 of *Eidos : Telos* (1995), the "sideways scene" in Forsythe's brilliant take on musical comedy *Isabelle's Dance* (1986)—all of these are part of the same vision of the world, in which the familiar is continually reconceived, and the unfamiliar repossesses the imagination.

Notes

1. Quoted in Sulcas, Roslyn (1995), "Kinetic Isometries", *Dance International*, Summer 1995, Vancouver
2. Confusingly for chronologers, Forsythe made a different ballet with the same name in 1987.

Figure 7   *Isabelle's Dance* (1986), Ballett Frankfurt
Photo: Charles Tandy © 1998

Choreography and Dance
2000, Vol. 5, Part 3, pp. 103–114
Photocopying permitted by license only

A Difficult and Lovely Work[1]

Steven Spier

The process of creating *Tight Roaring Circle*, a 1997 Artangel installation at The Roundhouse in London by Dana Caspersen, William Forsythe, and Joel Ryan, demonstrates their interest in working collaboratively and the issues it raises of authorship, disciplinary boundaries, and autonomy. In this instance the collaboration occurred not just among the credited creators, but with the curators and audience as well. While ostensibly light-hearted, *Tight Roaring Circle* was also a further exploration of engendering, ordering, and composing movement, issues also being pursued at Ballett Frankfurt, where Caspersen is a dancer and choreographer and for which Ryan often writes music.

KEY WORDS   Artangel, authenticity, collaboration, entrainment, installation, proprioperception, *Tight Roaring Circle*.

"When we [Artangel] start off a discussion with an artist there is no demand to know when a project will happen, what form it will take, where it will be, or how much it will cost. [The process] goes on for as long as it needs to. It seems to take two or three years, but there are some conversations which have been going on for longer than that and nothing concrete has emerged yet."[2] Michael Morris of Artangel[3] had long admired William Forsythe's work and his willingness to ignore boundaries between art forms, and felt that he was underrepresented in Britain.[4] He first approached Forsythe to do something with Artangel in 1993, though it was some time before they actually met. On 26 March 1997, four years after those overtures, *Tight Roaring Circle* opened in London, attributed in alphabetical order to Dana Caspersen, William Forsythe, and Joel Ryan, closing on 11 May 1997. Through it we shall see the issues raised by their decision to work collaboratively, and their interest in matters of authorship, engendering movement, and organizational principles.

Figure 1   The Roundhouse in London
All photos are of *Tight Roaring Circle*, Dana Caspersen, William Forsythe and Joel
Ryan, The Roundhouse, London NW1, March 26–May 11, 1997
Commissioned by Artangel
Photo © 1998 by Matthew Antrobus

Typically for Artangel, there were no preconceptions when they
approached Forsythe: "We don't start with anything, there are no
parameters. There is really just a table and not even a piece of paper
to start with. Just a conversation. And that's really how all these
commissions begin. It was really inviting, firstly, Forsythe, to sit
down and discuss a project."[5] Artangel does not simply commission a piece, then, but helps develop one. After agreeing to work
with them, Forsythe would be driven around London on his spor-
adic visits, being shown spaces that could be available for a temporary installation.[6] He then invited Caspersen to join him in
looking for "something with resonance."[7] Morris's choice of which
venues to show them was part of the creative process: "I would
take him to three or four places in a day, and each of those decisions
about where we would take him was motivated somehow by something he might have said in a conversation the night before. It was
like trying to pick up clues."[8] Just how open-ended the entire

process was is attested to by Morris: "In a way they are very unsentimental and they certainly taught myself and our production team to be unsentimental about good ideas."[9] Caspersen and Forsythe settled on The Roundhouse, a Grade II* listed [designated a moderately important historical building by English Heritage] locomotive shed designed by the London & North Western Railway's resident engineer, Robert Benson Dockray, and built in 1846–7. They later asked Ryan, a musician and designer of musical instruments who had worked with them on two recent pieces, to join them in creating an installation.

Working with such an open brief raised pragmatic issues, especially since Artangel is "funded just about to exist. Anything we want actually to do with our existence, we have to fund raise for. Now this project, all of our projects to some extent, we are fund raising in the dark."[10] With Caspersen *et al*. Artangel had to be even more nimble than usual: "The project changed shape, location, scale, and collaborative team all the way down the line", with the final decision on what the installation actually would be made approximately six weeks before the opening.[11] Moreover, fund raising had begun for earlier proposals, which posed a particular problem: "There is always a range of funding bodies; there is not just one investor to whom we have to say, oh by the way, it's changed, there are no dancers in it this week. So we have to time our update, which is delicate because we don't want the funding bodies to lose confidence in the project by every week saying, oh, there's no dancers, oh it's going to be this, oh it's going to be that. We had to time it really carefully and always put it forward as a very positive move and not that Billy's changed his mind again. Because that wasn't how it felt to us … I had a very difficult autumn, really worrying about this."[12] The only aspect Artangel was adamant about was the opening date: "That's the thing we would never, if you like, compromise on … Partly because I was aware that with Bill and Dana's schedule that if we missed the 24th of March 1997 it could be a year down the line, or way down the line."[13]

The Roundhouse is a huge, arresting space almost identical in size to the very large main stage in Frankfurt but with an elaborate, even ornate, nineteenth century cast iron structure.[14] Designed to stable and service locomotives, it had "24 radiating bays with a central turntable of 11m radius. Below each bay was a long pit which was used for maintenance and the removal of clinker …"[15] It was rendered technically obsolete within fifteen years of its construction as more powerful locomotives with larger boilers had to be made longer not higher due to the fixed circumference of tunnels and so could no longer fit onto the turntable. The building has acquired folkloric status as an object, has survived a panoply of uses and been the subject of almost countless proposals. For decades it was a gin warehouse for Gilbey's, later being used as a theater, rock music club, and arts venue.

The installation itself, though, was an inflated bouncy castle, like one would encounter at fun fairs or shopping malls, except that being the world's largest,[16] it occupied the entire middle space as defined by the colonnade. Soft, white, vinyl, and over-scaled with floppy castellations, the castle could not have stood out more from the patched brickwork and filigreed ironwork of the dour Roundhouse. It represents, of course, an archetype from childhood and a reference to Claes Oldenburg's floppy sculptures of the 1960s. But primarily it is a disarming, and rather silly, conceit, the figura-

Figure 2   The bouncy castle set within the colonnade of the Roundhouse
Artangel Commission
Photo © 1998 by Matthew Antrobus

tive nature of which, as against the expectations of a work commissioned from Forsythe by Artangel, disconcerted some critics.[17] Furthermore, given the venue and Forsythe's known interest in issues of the body in space, one might have imagined the space itself being the means and not just the setting, a more earnest, less figurative piece perhaps along the lines of James Turrell or Robert Irwin. The Roundhouse became important, though, less in abstract or historical terms than for its sheer vastness, and because, with its blind walls and the installation's evening opening hours, Caspersen *et al.* could use their expertise in theater and lighting to create an event.[18]

At the base of the short ramp by which one entered the castle was a wedge-shaped, gray-carpeted area with benches where one removed one's shoes. High up on each of its white interior walls was written in white a stanza from the following text:[19]

each passing year, never failing
to exact its toll
keeps altering what was sublime
into the stuff of comedy

is something eaten away

if the exterior is eaten away
is it true then that the sublime pertains by nature
only to an exterior
which conceals a core of nonsense

or
does the sublime indeed pertain to the whole,
but a ludicrous dust
settles upon it

There was a constant stream of partly live music, variously rhythmic, atmospheric, and melodic, with a fierce middle section bracketed by more structural, delicate ones. It was to refer non-narratively to The Roundhouse, its imaginative space as well as to the installation itself,[20] and to create "an atmosphere".[21]

In another context Forsythe has said that, "...Choreography should serve as a channel for the desire to dance."[22] In *Tight Roaring Circle* we were to share that passion and recapture the instinctive joy, the authentic impulse, the fearlessness with one's body that everyone has as a child, that time in one's life, as Forsythe puts it, when, "You are liberated from your fear of falling."[23] For in spite of

Figure 3   *Tight Roaring Circle*, with the text visible in the background
Artangel Commission
Photo © 1998 by Sarah Ainslie

the existing space, the inserted object, and the music, *Tight Roaring Circle* existed only through the animation of it by the participants, who were of all types and ages—the men in suits, the casually dressed, the old, the young, businesswomen, children. Some people took the opportunity to be more acrobatic than surely they can be in their everyday lives; others sat along the walls, resting, reading the text, listening to the music. A few lay in the middle to admire the building's roof. Others ran, hopped or skipped across; some bounced in place; others loped; some deliberately crashed into the walls. It functioned practically as a Rorschach test. One could not predict on any basis, generational, sartorial, class, race, or gender, how people would behave, though most behaved like children. There were even those few who refused to remove their shoes and enter it. It is one's congenitally diminishing sensation of the sublime that the elegiac text on the interior walls of the castle asks us to query.

Through the installation, Caspersen *et al.* were continuing their exploration of fundamental issues in choreography and perform-ance, and the theatrical, even enjoyable, aspect of *Tight Roaring*

Circle is one of them. Ryan states that a respect and necessity for the audience requires that they first be spellbound or captivated before they can be challenged.[24] Forsythe similarly acknowledges his responsibilities as artistic director and co-manager of what is a large, municipal company: "… most of the money we receive comes from taxes. It's not someone's private money. We're indebted to the community …"[25] But this responsibility does not necessarily mean pandering to the audience,[26] and *Tight Roaring Circle* does raise more conceptual issues concerning the body in space, and engendering and composing movement. For example, from the moment one stepped on to the inflated ramp to enter the castle, one's most taken-for-granted movements became mannered and thus noticeable. One was conscious of how much lighter the body can be, and reminded of that time when one's body seemed lighter. After exiting it reality felt very heavy indeed. But this awakened awareness of the body was not limited to the experience of gravity: "Another thing which happens is that people who are dancers engage in a lot of shifting alignments and they are used to being conscious of their alignment to other people. But people who are not dancers probably don't notice because it happens to such small degrees. But in the bouncy castle people will be delighted by their sudden disalignments and realignments."[27]

Because *Tight Roaring Circle* is animated by the public and not by professionals, and because Caspersen *et al.* don't assume even the role of editor, they are not faced with discovering or inventing mechanisms to hold diverse elements and people together lest a work become "just dancing around".[28] But the installation does nevertheless demonstrate what such means might be. "Choreography is about organizing bodies in space, or you're organizing bodies with other bodies, or a body with other bodies in an environment that is organized",[29] and for Caspersen and Forsythe the lack of collisions in *Tight Roaring Circle* is the manifestation of an ordering system, though as a self-organizing system it is an unusual hierarchy of voids and instincts.[30] Inside the castle, for example, the rules by which one defines spatial relationships with other people were at moments abruptly challenged by not being completely in control physically and by being encouraged to act without restraint. Even with the diminution of one's normal bearings, however, enough order was somehow maintained to allow everyone to act as he or she pleased, and, most critically, to avoid collisions.

Figure 4   *Tight Roaring Circle*
Artangel Commission
Photo © 1998 by Matthew Antrobus

If "Dancing is a conversation with gravity",[31] then *Tight Roaring Circle* is fundamentally a piece about dance itself and demonstrates in a simplified form some of the issues being pursued at Ballett Frankfurt. An appreciation of the profundity of an instinctive choreography as an organizing principle has lead Forsythe to investigate proprioperception and entrainment: "… I guess that when dancers are dancing, they are encountering an inner vision that can be described as the experience of proprioperception—the awareness of what one feels and sees one's body doing. And once you encounter this, you are opening yourself up to a whole lot of new information and new impulses that change one's dancing and approach to dance."[32] If proprioperception is about experiencing oneself, entrainment, "… the process that occurs when two or more people become engaged in each other's rhythms, when they synchronize,"[33] is about experiencing someone else. Caspersen and Forsythe borrow the concept from Edward T. Hall,[34] who argues that it is innate and metaphysical; at a quotidian level it is the phenomena, for example, that allow a conversation to happen—the pauses, nods, body language and sounds. In dance it draws on the dancer's own experience as well as talent and training, meaning that each performance is literally unique and cannot be notated: "You can probably notate, as a task, the outlines of the movement. You can't notate what has really happened because there are many moments that are simply a series of skeletal muscular reactions, a kind of inner refraction that is impossible to calculate and really notate. You can't even get it on video, because you lose a dimension. Often it's not even a question of the dance."[35]

Both proprioperception and entrainment ultimately rely on a dancer's authentic impulse,[36] his or her genuine participation. Antony Rizzi explains that, "Eventually the work comes from the dancers … no matter how, even if it ends up being that Billy [Forsythe] is just making a solo just for that person, at a certain point the work is left from Billy and now it's the dancer's. A lot of times Billy will say … when something's going, and the dancer hasn't developed the thing, especially to newer people, they don't understand, he's like 'I've given you a skeleton, always it's a skeleton, now you have to … fill it in'".[37] Forsythe has developed this idea to the extent that he now considers Ballett Frankfurt to be a choreographic ensemble,[38] and has in *Sleepers Guts* (1996) credited the choreographic themes to ten people. But, "It's not a democratic process. It's not like everyone in the company is equally gifted at choreography."[39] For, "This is not a concept of improvisation as an illusory freedom, nor of an anarchic free-for-all, but of a highly trained state in which dancers are able to rely on their own ability to access[40] appropriate movements for themselves and their contexts."[41]

Ultimately, "We organize a potential for interaction, as choreographers, which is also what we're doing here *[Tight Roaring Circle]*."[42] This potential exists not just between the choreographers and the audience, however. By collaborating so determinedly, distinctions among all the participants in all phases of the installation were diminished and confused. Caspersen says, "… it was as much Michael Morris and David Scofield's [production manager] piece as it was ours."[43] Forsythe also works closely with the managing director of Ballett Frankfurt, and finds him indispensable: "I am positive I wouldn't do this job without him [Martin Steinhoff]."[44] But working with Artangel, with so few parameters, requires tremendous respect amongst the collaborators. This takes time to gestate: "It's really building the foundations of the trust that will see you through two or three years of development. The whole thing ... is founded on trust."[45] Collaboration itself can take many forms, as Caspersen eloquently attests, and in *Tight Roaring Circle* they were attempting the most arduous: "There is the kind of collaboration where people work on different aspects of one project to create the whole, there is the kind where someone organizes the seminal parameters of an event and enables others [to] move into this field to find their own version of it, and then there is the kind of collaboration which is the coming together of two or more minds with the intent to carry out the difficult and lovely work of letting something take root and form in the expanded and complex space of minds thinking together about one task."[46]

Notes

1. This is a substantial revision of my article, "Organising the Organisation of Bodies in Space". *New Theatre Quarterly*, issue 55, summer 1998, Cambridge, England.
2. As quoted in Reynolds, Richard (1997) "Artangel" *Flash Art International* January/February 1997, p. 49, Milan.
3. Artangel "commissions and produces new, temporary works by contemporary artists. Each commission is shaped by its location ... and each project has at its centre the principle of collaboration" (Artangel's brochure). It was founded in 1985 and has been directed since 1991 by curators James Lingwood and Michael Morris. Its most famous commission has been "House", 1993–4, by Rachel Whiteread. Artangel is the topic of a forthcoming paper.
4. Michael Morris, interview with the author, London, 10 June 1997.
5. Ibid.
6. Dana Caspersen and William Forsythe, interview with the author, London, 25 March 1997.
7. From "A Conversation between Dana Caspersen, William Forsythe and the architect Daniel Libeskind" at the Royal Geographical Society, London, 7 March 1997. Professor Peter Cook substituted for an ill Libeskind.
8. Morris interview, op cit.
9. Ibid.
10. Ibid.
11. Ibid.
12. Ibid.
13. Ibid.
14. For a description see, "Important Works on the Birmingham Railway", *The Builder*, no. CCII, Saturday December 19, 1846, pp. 602–603, London.
15. Michael Hopkins and Partners, "British Architectural Library: Special Collections: The Roundhouse: Design Report" Heritage Lottery Fund Application, July 1995, p. 17.
16. *The Guinness Book of Records*, London: Guinness Publishing, 1997, p. 160. It stood 12m tall and 19m wide, was made of 2725 square meters of white PVC coated polyester, and took 15 minutes to fill with 385 cubic meters of air and 6 hours to erect fully.

17. For instance, see Searle, Adrian (1997) "Boing, Boing" *The Guardian*, 29 March 1997, p. 7, London, in which he concludes by saying, "Remember to take a small sharp object on your visit".

18. Caspersen and Forsythe interview, op. cit.

19. Mishima, Yukio (1973) *Runaway Horses* translated from the Japanese by Michael Gallagher, London: Martin Secker & Warburg Limited, 1973, p. 214. The actual quote is prose. The same text is used in Forsythe's *Loss of Small Detail*.

20. Joel Ryan, telephone interview with the author, London, 14 June 1997.

21. Caspersen, Forsythe and Libeskind, op. cit.

22. Sulcas, Roslyn (1995) "Kinetic Isometries: William Forsythe on his 'continuous rethinking of the ways in which movement can be engendered and composed'", *Dance International*, Summer 1995, p. 8, Vancouver.

23. Bruce, Nichola, (director) (1998) *Tight Roaring Circle: Dana Caspersen, William Forsythe, Joel Ryan*, part of the Artangel Afterlives video series, London: Artangel, 1998.

24. Ryan, op cit.

25. Driver, Senta & the editors of Ballet Review (1990) "A Conversation with William Forsythe", *Ballet Review*, 18.1, Spring 1990, p. 87, New York.

26. A Ballett Frankfurt piece, for example, can be described visually as such: "… moving through ballet like a fish through water as it disregards the conventional logic that governs the order and impulses of steps, incorporating infinite planes of orientation. Legs buckle, bottoms push back, arms skew, classical lines are drawn and erased in the air or on the floor. A finger determines momentum and direction; an ear leads the body as it writes in space; verticality and effortlessness appear and vanish like the imaginary constructs they are." From Sulcas, Roslyn (1997) "In the News: The Continuing Evolution of Mr. Forsythe" *Dance Magazine* January 1997, p. 35, New York. The pieces are demanding in their athleticism.

27. Dana Caspersen in Bruce, op cit.

28. Figgis, Mike (director) (1996) *"Just Dancing Around?: Bill Forsythe"*, Channel Four version, Euphoria Films, 50'59" 1996. Aired 27 December 1996, Channel Four, 19.30, Great Britain.

29. Caspersen, Forsythe and Libeskind, op. cit.; Figgis, op. cit.

30. Caspersen and Forsythe interview, op. cit. He remarked that during a preview the night before its opening, there were 50 children inside and no collisions.

31. Caspersen, Forsythe, and Libeskind, op. cit.

32. Sulcas, Roslyn (1995) "Kinetic Isometries", op. cit., p. 7.

33. Caspersen, Forsythe and Libeskind, op. cit.

34. See Hall, Edward T., *The Dance of Life, The Other Dimension of Time*, New York: Anchor Books/Doubleday, 1983.

35. Sulcas, Roslyn (1995) "Kinetic Isometries", op. cit., p. 8.

36. Caspersen and Forsythe interview, op. cit.

37. Figgis, Mike (1996) op cit. Rizzi is a choreographer and dancer with the company.

38. Caspersen, Forsythe and Libeskind, op. cit.

39. Caspersen and Forsythe interview, op. cit.

40. In correspondence with the author Forsythe changed this verb from "create".

41. Sulcas, Roslyn (1991) "Poetry of Disappearance" *Dance Theatre Journal* 9, 1, summer 1991, p. 33, London.

42. Caspersen and Forsythe interview, op. cit.

43. Caspersen, fax to the author, 13 July 1997.

44. Figgis, Mike (1996) op. cit. Steinhoff, who regards Forsythe as a genius and a friend, states his perceived predicament in working collaboratively with an artist: "Artists need a kind of partner. They don't need a slave. They always want a slave. They want to have somebody who is solving their problems, helping them in being successful, but who they can treat as they want." Forsythe cites their ability to argue with each other as a key to their relationship.
45. Morris interview, op. cit.
46. Caspersen fax, op. cit.

Choreography and Dance
2000, Vol. 5, Part 3, pp. 115–126
Photocopying permitted by license only

Chronological and Alphabetical Lists of Forsythe Works

compiled by Senta Driver with research assistance from
Rainer Woihsyk, archivist of the Stuttgart Ballet,
and Anne Midgette

Where a ballet has been known by more than one title, it is listed under the one used in 1998 Ballett Frankfurt records. Many Forsythe works are constructed in sections that are individually named, with separate scores and design teams. These sections have frequently been premiered before the larger work into which they move, and Forsythe often continues to present them on their own. Such works are included below under their own titles, with indication of the parent work.

1976 *Urlicht*, duet for William Forsythe and Eileen Brady, Noverre Society, Stuttgart
    music by Gustav Mahler, *Urlicht*; text from *Des Knaben Wunderhorn*

1977 *Daphne*, Stuttgart Ballet, Stuttgart
    music by Antonin Dvořák, *Symphony No. 7 in D Minor*, 2nd and 3rd movements
    Bach Violin Concerto in A Minor, Basel Ballet, Basel
    music by Johann Sebastian Bach, *Violin Concerto in A Minor*
    Flore Subsimplici, Stuttgart Ballet, Stuttgart
    music by Georg Friedrich Händel, *Concerti Grossi Op. 6, No. 7, 2, 5*
    stage and costume design by William Forsythe

1978 *From the Most Distant Time/In Endloser Zeit*, Stuttgart Ballet, Stuttgart

music by Györgi Ligeti, *Double Concerto for Flute and Oboe*
stage, lighting, and costume design by Arthur Brady
Dream of Galilei/Traum des Galilei, Stuttgart Ballet, Stuttgart
music by Krzysztof Penderecki, *Symphony No. 1*
Folia/Folia Espagnola, Stuttgart Ballet, Montepulciano Festival,
Italy
music by Hans Werner Henze, *Aria de la Folia Espagnola*
1979   *Orpheus*, Stuttgart Ballet, Stuttgart
music by Hans Werner Henze; libretto by Edward Bond
stage design by Axel Manthey; costumes by Joachim Herzog
Love Songs/Side 2—Love Songs/Seite 1—Love Song—Alte Platten
[original title *Love Songs—Part 1 Seite 1; part 2 Love Songs;*
part 3 Alte Platten], Stuttgart Ballet, Munich
music: Aretha Franklin and Dionne Warwick
stage and lighting design by William Forsythe; costumes
by Eileen Brady
Time Cycle, Stuttgart Ballet, Stuttgart
music by Lukas Foss, *Time Cycle, Song Cycle for Soprano and*
Orchestra to texts by Auden, Housman, Kafka, and Nietzsche
stage design and costumes by Axel Manthey; lighting by
Joop Caboort
1980   *Joyleen Gets Up, Gets Down, Goes Out*, Bavarian State Opera
Ballet, Munich
music by Boris Blacher, *Blues, Espagnola und Rumba philhar-*
monica für 12 violoncelli soli
costumes by Eileen Brady
'Tis Pity She's a Whore/Schade dass sie eine Hure ist, Stuttgart
Ballet, Montepulciano Festival, Italy
music by Thomas Jahn; libretto after John Ford's 17th
century play
stage and costume design by Randi Bubat; lighting by
Hanns-Joachim Haas
Famous Mothers Club, solo for Lynn Seymour, London
music by David Cunningham
Say Bye Bye, Nederlands Dans Theater, The Hague, The
Netherlands
music collage of rock and popular music arranged by
William Forsythe and orchestrated by Jürgen Vater
stage design by Axel Manthey; costumes by Eileen Brady
and Axel Manthey
1981   *Die Nacht aus Blei/Night of Lead/Nacht aus dem Blei,*

Ballet Deutsche Oper, Berlin
music by Hans-Jürgen von Bose; libretto by Hans Henny Jahnn
stage design by Axel Manthey
Whisper Moon, Stuttgart Ballet, Stuttgart
music by William Bolcom, *Quintet for Violin, Violoncello, Flute, Clarinet and Piano*
stage design and costumes by Axel Manthey
Tancredi and Clorinda, Stuttgart Ballet, Stuttgart
music: montage

1982   *Gänge 1—Ein Stück Über Ballett*, Nederlands Dans Theater, The Hague, The Netherlands
music electronic collage by William Forsythe
stage design by Michael Simon; costumes by Tom Schenk

1983   *Gänge—Stück von William Forsythe und Michael Simon* [full length version], Ballett Frankfurt, Frankfurt
music by Thomas Jahn
stage design by William Forsythe and Michael Simon; costumes by Randi Bubat, Ingolf Thiel, and Tom Schenk
Mental Model, Nederlands Dans Theater, The Hague, The Netherlands
music by Igor Stravinsky, *Quatre Études pour Orchestre, Four Norwegian Moods, Scherzo á la Russe*
stage design by William Forsythe; lighting by William Forsythe and Joop Caboort; costumes by Stephen Meha
Square Deal, Joffrey Ballet, New York
composition and visual effects by William Forsythe
music by William Forsythe and Thomas Jahn
lighting by Jennifer Tipton; costumes by Douglas Furgusan
France/Dance, Paris Opéra Ballet, Paris
music by Johann Sebastian Bach, arranged by William Forsythe
stage and costume design by Cara Perlman and William Forsythe; objects by Cara Perlman; lighting by William Forsythe

1984   *Berg ab/Downhill* [title at premiere was *Three Orchestral Pieces—a Motion Picture*], film for the Vienna State Opera Ballet, Vienna
music by Alban Berg, *Three Orchestral Pieces # 6*
technical collaboration: Alida Chase, Cara Perlman, Gerhard Benz, Marcus Spies, and Ronald Thornhill

Artifact, Ballett Frankfurt, Frankfurt
music by Johann Sebastian Bach, *Chaconne* from *Partita #2 in D minor for Solo Violin* with free variations by Eva Crossman-Hecht; text by William Forsythe
stage, lighting, and costume design by William Forsythe
Steptext, Aterballetto, Reggio Emilia, Italy
music by Johann Sebastian Bach, *Chaconne* from *Partita #2 in D minor for Solo Violin*
stage, lighting, and costume design by William Forsythe

1985   *LDC*, Ballett Frankfurt, Frankfurt
music by Thom Willems
stage design by Michael Simon; lighting by William Forsythe; costumes by Benedikt Ramm

1986   *Isabelle's Dance*, Ballett Frankfurt, Frankfurt
music by Eva Crossman-Hecht; lyrics by Eva Crossman-Hecht, William Forsythe, Sara Neece, and Stephen Saugey
stage design by Michael Simon; costumes by Férial Simon
Skinny, Ballett Frankfurt, Frankfurt
choreography by William Forsythe and Amanda Miller
music by Thom Willems and William Forsythe; text by William Forsythe and Kathleen Fitzgerald
stage and lighting design by William Forsythe; costumes by William Forsythe and Amanda Miller
Die Befragung des Robert Scott/The Questioning of Robert Scott, Ballett Frankfurt, Frankfurt
music by Thom Willems
stage and lighting design by William Forsythe; costumes by William Forsythe and Holly Brubach
Big White Baby Dog, Ballett Frankfurt, Frankfurt
music by Thom Willems; text by Anne Waldman from *Empty Speech*
stage and lighting design by William Forsythe; costumes by William Forsythe and Holly Brubach
Baby Sam, Ballett Frankfurt, Bari, Italy
music by Thom Willems
Pizza Girl (Ninety One-Minute Ballets), Ballett Frankfurt, Frankfurt
choreography by Alida Chase, William Forsythe, Stephen Galloway, Timothy Gordon, Dieter Heitkamp, Evan Jones, Amanda Miller, Vivienne Newport, Cara Perlman, Benedikt

Ramm, Antony Rizzi, Ana Cataline Roman, Iris Tenge, Ron
Thornhill, Berna Uythov, Thom Willems
    music by Thom Willems
    stage design by Benedikt Ramm; painting *Pizza Girl* by
    Cara Perlman

1987   *New Sleep*, San Francisco Ballet, San Francisco
    music by Thom Willems
    stage and costume design by William Forsythe and
    Benedikt Ramm; lighting by William Forsythe
   Same Old Story, Ballett Frankfurt, Hamburg
    music by Thom Willems; text by Kathleen Fitzgerald,
    Nicholas Champion, and William Forsythe
    stage, lighting, and costume design by William Forsythe
   The Loss of Small Detail, Ballett Frankfurt, Frankfurt (recon-
   ceived 1991 version incorporates *the second detail*)
    music by Thom Willems
    stage design by William Forsythe; costumes by Issey
    Miyake and William Forsythe
   In the Middle, Somewhat Elevated, Paris Opéra Ballet, Paris
   (later incorporated into *Impressing the Czar*)
    direction and choreography by William Forsythe
    music by Thom Willems, Leslie Stuck
    stage design by Michael Simon; lighting by William
    Forsythe
    costumes by William Forsythe and Férial Simon

1988   *Impressing the Czar*, Ballett Frankfurt, Frankfurt (incorporates
   In the Middle, Somewhat Elevated)
    music by Ludwig van Beethoven, *String Quartet #14 opus
    131 in C# minor*, Leslie Stuck, Thom Willems, Eva
    Crossman-Hecht
    stage design by Michael Simon; lighting by William
    Forsythe and Michael Simon; costumes by Férial Simon
   Behind the China Dogs, New York City Ballet, New York
    music by Leslie Stuck
    china dogs by Cara Perlman; lighting by Mark Stanley;
    costumes by William Forsythe and Barbara Matera
   The Vile Parody of Address, Ballett Frankfurt, Frankfurt
    music by Johann Sebastian Bach, *Well-Tempered Clavier*
    played by Glenn Gould; text by William Forsythe;
    "paroles" by Nicholas Champion
    stage, lighting, and costume design by William Forsythe

1989   *Enemy in the Figure*, Ballett Frankfurt, Frankfurt (later incorporated into *Limb's Theorem*)
    music by Thom Willems
    stage, lighting, and costume design by William Forsythe
    Slingerland Teil I, Ballett Frankfurt, Frankfurt
    music by Gavin Bryars, *String Quartet #1, Three Viennese Dancers*
    film and stage design by Cara Perlman and William Forsythe; lighting and costumes by William Forsythe

1990   *Limb's Theorem*, Ballett Frankfurt, Frankfurt (incorporates *Enemy in the Figure*)
    conceptual collaboration by Heidi Gilpin
    music by Thom Willems
    stage and lighting design by Michael Simon and William Forsythe; costumes by Férial Simon
    Slingerland Teil II and III, Ballett Frankfurt, Amsterdam [Teil II and III later became Acts III and IV]
    music by Gavin Bryars, *String Quartet*, and Thom Willems
    film and stage design by Cara Perlman and William Forsythe; lighting and costumes by William Forsythe
    Slingerland Teil IV, Ballett Frankfurt, Paris
    music by Thom Willems
    film and stage design by Cara Perlman and William Forsythe; lighting and costumes by William Forsythe

1991   *the second detail*, National Ballet of Canada, Toronto (incorporated 1991 into *The Loss of Small Detail*)
    music by Thom Willems
    stage and lighting design by William Forsythe; costumes by Issey Miyake and William Forsythe
    Marion/Marion, Nederlands Dans Theater 3, The Hague, The Netherlands
    music by Bernard Herrmann
    The Loss of Small Detail—neufassung, Ballett Frankfurt, Frankfurt
    (substantially reconceived; incorporates *the second detail*)
    music by Thom Willems; text by William Forsythe, Yukio Mushima, and Jérôme Rothenberg
    film by Helga Fanderl and Fiona Léus; film animation by Huntley/Muir of London; photography by Dominik Mentzos; stage and lighting design by William Forsythe; costumes by Issey Miyake

Snap. Woven Effort, Ballett Frankfurt, Frankfurt
music by Thom Willems; text by William Forsythe, Dana Caspersen, David Kern, Mark Adam, Helen Pickett, Christine Bürkle, and Stephen Galloway
stage and lighting design by William Forsythe; costumes by Gianni Versace

1992   *As a Garden in This Setting, Part I*, Ballett Frankfurt, Frankfurt
music by Thom Willems; dramaturgie by Steven Valk
video by Sean Toren; stage and lighting design by William Forsythe; costumes by Issey Miyake and Naoki Takizawa

Herman Schmerman, New York City Ballet, New York
music by Thom Willems
production design by William Forsythe; lighting by Mark Stanley; costumes by Gianni Versace and William Forsythe

A L I E /N A(C)TION, Ballett Frankfurt, Frankfurt
music by Thom Willems, Arnold Schönberg; dramaturgie by Steven Valk
video by Sean Toren; stage and lighting design by William Forsythe; costumes by Stephen Galloway

1993   *Quintett*, Ballett Frankfurt, Frankfurt
choreography by William Forsythe with Dana Caspersen, Stephen Galloway, Jacopo Godani, Thomas McManus, and Jone San Martin
music by Gavin Bryars, *Jesus' Blood Never Failed Me Yet*
stage and lighting design by William Forsythe; costumes by Stephen Galloway

As a Garden in This Setting, Teil II (and Through Them Filters Futile), Ballett Frankfurt, Frankfurt
music by Thom Willems; dramaturgie by Steven Valk
video by Sean Toren; costumes by Issey Miyake and Naoki Takizawa

1994   *Self Meant to Govern/Selbsternannt zum Regieren*, Ballett Frankfurt, Frankfurt (later incorporated into *Eidos : Telos*)
music by Thom Willems and Maxim Franke
stage and lighting design by William Forsythe; costumes by Stephen Galloway

Pivot House, Ballett Frankfurt, Reggio Emilia, Italy
music by Kraton Surakarta
video by Richard Caon; stage and lighting design by William Forsythe; costumes by Stephen Galloway

1995   *Eidos : Telos*, Ballett Frankfurt, Frankfurt (incorporates *Self Meant to Govern*)
concept and organization by William Forsythe in choreographic association with the ensemble
> music by Thom Willems and Joel Ryan; text by William Forsythe and Roberto Colasso; monologue by Dana Caspersen; dramaturgical research by Heidi Gilpin
> video by Richard Caon; costumes by Stephen Galloway and Naoki Takizawa (Miyake Design Studio)
> computer programming by Michael Saup

Firstext, The Royal Ballet, London
choreography by Dana Caspersen, William Forsythe, and Antony Rizzi
> music by Thom Willems
> stage design by William Forsythe; costumes by Naoki Takizawa (Miyake Design Studio) and Raymond Dragon Design Inc.

Invisible Film, Ballett Frankfurt, Frankfurt
> music by Johann Sebastian Bach, Georg Friedrich Händel, Henry Purcell; text by William Forsythe and Parliament
> stage and lighting design by William Forsythe; costumes by Stephen Galloway

Of Any If And, Ballett Frankfurt, Frankfurt
> music by Thom Willems; text by William Forsythe and Dana Caspersen
> stage and lighting design by William Forsythe; costumes by Stephen Galloway

Four Point Counter, Nederlands Dans Theater, The Hague, The Netherlands (later incorporated into *Six Counter Points*)
> music by Thom Willems
> stage and lighting design by William Forsythe; costumes by Stephen Galloway

The The (later incorporated into *Six Counter Points*) duet for Anne Affourtit and Derek Brown, Holland Festival, The Hague, The Netherlands
choreography by Dana Caspersen and William Forsythe
> no music
> stage and lighting design by William Forsythe; costumes by Stephen Galloway and Dawn Aronson

Solo, William Forsythe for the video *Evidentia*, conceived by Sylvie Guillem and produced by RD Studio Productions, France 2/BBC
> direction by Thomas Lovell Balogh
> music by Thom Willems
> director of photography: Jess Hall

1996 *Six Counter Points*, Ballett Frankfurt, Frankfurt (incorporates *Four Point Counter* and *The The*, and adds the following four works, all later presented as independent pieces:
Duo
> music by Thom Willems
> stage, lighting, and costume design by William Forsythe

Trio
> music by Ludwig van Beethoven, *String Quartet #15 in A minor, opus 132* and Alban Berg, *Quartett*
> stage and lighting design by William Forsythe; costumes by Stephen Galloway

Approximate Sonata/one of *Two Ballets in the Manner of the Late 20th Century*
> music by Thom Willems and Tricky Pumpkin
> stage and lighting design by William Forsythe; costumes by Stephen Galloway

The Vertiginous Thrill of Exactitude/one of *Two Ballets in the Manner of the Late 20th Century*
> music by Franz Schubert, *Symphony #9 in C Major, allegro vivace*
> stage and lighting design by William Forsythe; costumes by Stephen Galloway

Sleepers Guts—Ein Stück des Ballett Frankfurt, Ballett Frankfurt, Frankfurt
primary choreographic material (Choreographische Hauptthematik): William Forsythe, Jacopo Godani, Antony Rizzi, Ion Garnika, Francesca Caroti, Christine Bürkle, Agnès Noltenius, Marc Spradling, Alan Barnes, Francesca Harper, Bahiyah Sayyed. Choreography of Part 3 by Jacopo Godani
> music by Thom Willems and Joel Ryan
> video by Bill Seaman; stage and lighting design by William Forsythe; costumes by Stephen Galloway

Hypothetical Stream, Compagnie Daniel Larrieu, Tours, France

music by Stuart Dempster, *Standing Waves*, and Ingram
Marshall, *Fog Tropes*
stage and lighting design by William Forsythe; costumes
by Raymond Dragon and Simon Frearson

1997   *Tight Roaring Circle*, installation for Artangel, London
created by William Forsythe with Dana Caspersen
music by Joel Ryan
From a Classical Position, Dana Caspersen and William
Forsythe for Euphoria Films, Channel Four, London
direction and choreography for video by William Forsythe
with Dana Caspersen
music by Thom Willems
director of photography: Jess Hall
costumes by Stephen Galloway
Hypothetical Stream 2, Ballett Frankfurt, Frankfurt
choreography by William Forsythe and Regina van Berkel,
Christine Bürkle, Ana Catalina Roman, Jone San Martin,
Timothy Couchman, Noah Gelber, Jacopo Godani, Antony
Rizzi, Richard Siegal
music by Stuart Dempster, *Standing Waves*, and Ingram
Marshall, *Fog Tropes*
stage and lighting design by William Forsythe; costumes
by Stephen Galloway

1998   *small void*, Ballett Frankfurt, Frankfurt
choreography by William Forsythe in collaboration with
Stefanie Arndt, Alan Barnes, Dana Caspersen, Noah Gelber,
Anders Hellström, Fabrice Mazliah, Tamás Moritz, Crystal
Pite, Jone San Martin, Richard Siegal, Pascal Touzeau, and
Sjored Vreugdenhil
music by Thom Willems
stage and lighting design by William Forsythe; costumes
by Stephen Galloway
op. 31, (erste Fassungen)
music by Arnold Schoenberg, *Variations for Orchestra op. 31*
stage and lighting design by William Forsythe; costumes
by Stephen Galloway

Alphabetical list

Alphabetical ordering of ballets using more than one title follows the title used in Ballett Frankfurt records

A L I E /N A(C)TION (1992)
Approximate Sonata (1996)
Artifact (1984)
As a Garden in This Setting, Part I (1992)
As a Garden in This Setting, Teil II (and Through Them Filters Futile) (1993)
Baby Sam (1986)
Bach Violin Concerto in A Minor (1977)
Behind the China Dogs (1988)
Berg ab/Downhill [title at premiere was *Three Orchestral Pieces—a Motion Picture*] (1984)
Big White Baby Dog (1986)
Daphne (1977)
Die Befragung des Robert Scott/The Questioning of Robert Scott (1986)
Die Nacht aus Blei/Night of Lead/Nacht aus dem Blei (1981)
Dream of Galilei/Traum des Galilei (1978)
Duo (1996)
Eidos : Telos (1995)
Enemy in the Figure (1989)
Famous Mothers Club (1980)
Firstext (1995)
Flore Subsimplici (1977)
Folia/Folia Espagnola (1978)
Four Point Counter (1995)
France/Dance (1983)
From a Classical Position (1997)
From the Most Distant Time/In Endloser Zeit (1978)
Gänge 1—Ein Stück Über Ballett (1982)
Gänge—Stück von William Forsythe und Michael Simon (1983)
Herman Schmerman (1992)
Hypothetical Stream (1996)
Hypothetical Stream 2 (1997)
Impressing the Czar (1988)
In the Middle, Somewhat Elevated (1987)
Invisible Film (1995)
Isabelle's Dance (1986)

Joyleen Gets Up, Gets Down, Goes Out (1980)
LDC (1985)
Limb's Theorem (1990)
Love Songs/Side 2—Love Songs/Seite 1—Love Song—Alte Platten/Love Songs—Old Records (1979)
Marion/Marion (1991)
Mental Model (1983)
New Sleep (1987)
Of Any If And (1995)
op. 31, (erste Fassungen) (1998)
Orpheus (1979)
Pivot House (1994)
Pizza Girl (Ninety One-Minute Ballets) (1986)
Quintett (1993)
Same Old Story (1987)
Say Bye Bye (1980)
Self Meant to Govern/Selbsternannt zum Regieren (1994)
Six Counter Points (1996)
Skinny (1986)
Sleepers Guts, ein Stück des Ballett Frankfurt (1996)
Slingerland Teil I (1989)
Slingerland Teil II and III (1990)
Slingerland Teil IV (1990)
small void (1998)
Snap. Woven Effort (1991)
Solo (1995)
Square Deal (1983)
Steptext (1984)
Tancredi and Clorinda (1981)
The Loss of Small Detail/Loss of Small Detail (1987/reconceived 1991)
the second detail (1991)
The The (1995)
The Vertiginous Thrill of Exactitude (1996)
The Vile Parody of Address (1988)
Tight Roaring Circle (1997)
Time Cycle (1979)
'Tis Pity She's a Whore/Schade dass sie eine Hure ist (1980)
Trio (1996)
Urlicht (1976)
Whisper Moon (1981)

Choreography and Dance
2000, Vol. 5, Part 3, pp. 127–128
Photocopying permitted by license only

Notes on Contributors

Dana Caspersen grew up in Minneapolis, Minnesota, attended the Children's Theater School there, and later studied with Maggie Black and Erick Hawkins, among other teachers. She performed for three years with the North Carolina Dance Theater before joining the Frankfurt Ballet in 1987.

In Frankfurt she has contributed to and created numerous works as a dancer, actress, author, and choreographer. She has collaborated on several projects with William Forsythe, including *Firstext* for the Royal Ballet, *The The* for the Frankfurt Ballet, her extended monologue in *Eidos : Telos*, the film *From a Classical Position* for British television's Channel Four, and the site-specific installation *Tight Roaring Circle* for Artangel in London. In 1998 Caspersen premiered her first solo projects, *Work #1*, choreographed for Sylvie Guillem and Michael Schumacher, and *Work #2*, created for the Frankfurt Ballet.

Senta Driver danced with the Paul Taylor Company from 1967–1973 and made dance and other works for her own company, HARRY, for 16 years from 1975. During that time she also served as panelist and juror for The National Endowment for the Arts, the New York and Pennsylvania State Arts Councils, and numerous private foundations and festivals. She was a Guggenheim Fellow for 1978, sat on the Board of Directors and the Executive Committee of Dance/USA, and has published articles and reviews in *Dance Scope, Ballet Review,* and the journal of the Dance Critics' Association. She has been covering William Forsythe since 1988, chiefly for *Ballet Review,* and met Dana Caspersen when mounting *Resettings* on the North Carolina Dance Theater, with Caspersen in the cast.

Anne Midgette is a long-time European correspondent for the Leisure and Arts page of the *Wall Street Journal* and *Opera News*. She also writes about opera, theater, music, and the visual arts for the *New York Times, Newsday, Opern Welt*, and other publications. During 11 years of residence in Munich one of her fields of specialization was arts funding, which she has covered in major articles for *Opera News, The Wall Street Journal*, and the *New York Times*. A Yale graduate in Classical Civilizations, she now lives in New York, where she continues as a writer and cultural critic. She has also published travel guidebooks for destinations in Germany, the United States, the United Kingdom, France, and Greece.

Steven Spier has lived since late 1994 in London, where he is a lecturer in architecture at South Bank University, teaching design. He is currently researching Forsythe's relationship to Laban and his notation system, and the subject of drawing conventions in architecture. In addition, he writes on contemporary architecture, mostly from the German-speaking world, for the academic and professional press. He was raised in New Jersey, received a Bachelor's degree in philosophy from Haverford College outside Philadelphia, and afterwards worked in New York City in television advertising and book publishing. He then lived in Los Angeles for six years, where he received a Master's degree in architecture from the Southern California Institute of Architecture in Los Angeles, and worked in architectural practice. He has since lived and practiced architecture in Berlin and in Zurich.

Roslyn Sulcas is from Cape Town, South Africa, where she danced briefly before pursuing a Masters degree in literature at the University of Cape Town, and a doctorate at York University in England and then Paris VII. The first Ballett Frankfurt season in Paris moved her to begin writing about dance, and she became the Paris correspondent of *Dance and Dancers* and *Dance Magazine*, also working in the publications department of the Paris Opéra Ballet. Sulcas moved to New York in 1996. Her work appears in *Dance Magazine, Dance International, Dance Now*, the *New York Times, Elle*, and *Stagebill*. She is currently working on a book about William Forsythe.

Choreography and Dance
2000, Vol. 5, Part 3, pp. 129–131
Photocopying permitted by license only

Index

[italics denote illustrations]

CHOREOGRAPHY AND DANCE
AN INTERNATIONAL JOURNAL

Notes for contributors

Submission of a paper will be taken to imply that it represents original work not previously published, that it is not being considered for publication elsewhere and that, if accepted for publication, it will not be published elsewhere in the same form, in any language, without the consent of editor and publisher. It is a condition of acceptance by the editor of a typescript for publication that the publisher automatically acquires the copyright of the typescript throughout the world. It will also be assumed that the author has obtained all necessary permissions to include in the paper items such as quotations, musical examples, figures, tables etc. Permissions should be paid for prior to submission.

Typescripts. Papers should be submitted in triplicate to the Editors, *Choreography and Dance*, c/o Harwood Academic Publishers, at:

5th Floor, Reading Bridge House	PO Box 32160	3-14-9, Okubo
Reading Bridge Approach	Newark	Shinjuku-ku
Reading RG1 8PP	NJ 07102	Tokyo 169-0072
UK or	USA or	Japan

Papers should be typed or word processed with double spacing on one side of good quality ISO A4 (212 × 297mm) paper with a 3cm left-hand margin. Papers are accepted only in English.

Abstracts and Keywords. Each paper requires an abstract of 100–150 words summarizing the significant coverage and findings, presented on a separate sheet of paper. Abstracts should be followed by up to six key words or phrases which, between them, should indicate the subject matter of the paper. These will be used for indexing and data retrieval purposes.

Figures. All figures (photographs, schema, charts, diagrams and graphs) should be numbered with consecutive arabic numerals, have descriptive captions and be mentioned in the text. Figures should be kept separate from the text but an approximate position for each should be indicated in the margin of the typescript. It is the author's responsibility to obtain permission for any reproduction from other sources.

Preparation: Line drawings must be of a high enough standard for direct reproduction; photocopies are not acceptable. They should be prepared in black (india) ink on white art paper, card or tracing paper, with all the lettering and symbols included. Computer-generated graphics of a similar high quality are also acceptable, as are good sharp photoprints ("glossie"). Computer print-outs must be completely legible. Photographs intended for halftone reproduction must be good glossy original prints of maximum contrast. Redrawing or retouching of unusable figures will be charged to authors.

Size: Figures should be planned so that they reduce to 12cm column width. The preferred width of line drawings is 24cm, with capital lettering 4mm high, for reduction by one-half. Photographs for halftone reproduction should be approximately twice the desired finished size.

Captions: A list of figure captions, with the relevant figure numbers, should be typed on a separate sheet of paper and included with the typescript.

Musical examples: Musical examples should be designated as "Figure 1" etc., and the recommendations above for preparation and sizing should be followed. Examples must be well prepared and of a high standard for reproduction, as they will not be redrawn or retouched by the printer.

In the case of large scores, musical examples will have to be reduced in size and so some clarity will be lost. This should be borne in mind especially with orchestral scores.

Notes are indicated by superior arabic numerals without parentheses. The text of the notes should be collected at the end of the paper.

References are indicated in the text by the name and date system either "Recent work (Smith & Jones, 1987, Robinson, 1985, 1987)..." or "Recently Smith & Jones (1987)..." If a publication has more than three authors, list all names on the first occurrence; on subsequent occurrences use the first author's name plus *et al*. Use an ampersand rather than "and" between the last two authors. If there is more than one publication by the same author(s) in the same year, distinguish by adding a, b, c etc. to both the text citation and the list of references (e.g. "Smith, 1986a"). References should be collected and typed in alphabetical order after the Notes and Acknowledgements sections (if these exist). Examples:

Benedetti, J. (1988) Stanislavski, London: Methuen.

Granville-Barker, H. (1934) Shakespeare's dramatic art. In *A Companion to Shakespeare Studies*, edited by H. Granville-Barker and G.B. Harrison, p. 84. Cambridge: Cambridge University Press

Johnson, D. (1970) Policy in theatre. Hibernia, 16, 16.

Proofs. Authors will receive page proofs (including figures) by air mail for correction and these must be returned as instructed within 48hours of receipt. Please ensure that a full postal address is given on the first page of the typescript so that proofs are not delayed in the post. Authors' alterations, other than those of a typographical nature, in excess of 10% of the original composition cost, will be charged to authors.

Page Charges. There are no page charges to individuals or institutions.

INSTRUCTIONS FOR AUTHORS

ARTICLE SUBMISSION ON DISK

The Publisher welcomes submissions on disk. The instructions that follow are intended for use by authors whose articles have been accepted for publication and are in final form. Your adherence to these guidelines will facilitate the processing of your disk by the typesetter. These instructions do not replace the journal Notes for Contributors; all information in Notes for Contributors remains in effect.

When typing your article, do not include design or formatting information. Type all text flush left, unjustified and without hyphenation. Do not use indents, tabs or multi-spacing. If an indent is required, please note it by a line space; also mark the position of the indent on the hard copy manuscript. Indicate the beginning of a new paragraph by typing a line space. Leave one space at the end of a sentence, after a comma or other punctuation mark, and before an opening parenthesis. Be sure not to confuse lower case letter "l" with numeral "1", or capital letter "O" with numeral "0". Distinguish opening quotes from close quotes. Do not use automatic page numbering or running heads.

Tables and displayed equations may have to be rekeyed by the typesetter from your hard copy manuscript. Refer to the journal Notes for Contributors for style for Greek characters, variables, vectors, etc.

Articles prepared on most word processors are acceptable. If you have imported equations and/or scientific symbols into your article from another program, please provide details of the program used and the procedures you followed. If you have used macros that you have created, please include them as well.

You may supply illustrations that are available in an electronic format on a separate disk. Please clearly indicate on the disk the file format and/or program used to produce them, and supply a high-quality hard copy of each illustration as well.

Submit your disk when you submit your final hard copy manuscript. The disk file and hard copy must match exactly.

If you are submitting more than one disk, please number each disk. Please mark each disk with the journal title, author name, abbreviated article title and file names.

Be sure to retain a back-up copy of each disk submitted. Pack your disk carefully to avoid damage in shipping, and submit it with your hard copy manuscript and complete Disk Specifications form (see reverse) to the person designated in the journal Notes for Contributors.

Disk Specifications

Journal name _____

_____

Date _____ Paper Reference Number _____

Paper title_____

_____

_____

Corresponding author _____

Address_____

_____

_____

_____ Postcode _____

Telephone _____

Fax _____

E-mail_____

Disks Enclosed (file names and descriptions of contents)

Text

Disk 1 _____

Disk 2 _____

Disk 3 _____

PLEASE RETAIN A BACK-UP COPY OF ALL DISK FILES SUBMITTED.

GORDON AND BREACH PUBLISHERS • **HARWOOD ACADEMIC PUBLISHERS**

Figures

Disk 1 _____

Disk 2 _____

Disk 3 _____

Computer make and model_____

_____

Size/format of floppy disks

☐ 3.5"　　　　　　☐ 5.25"

☐ Single sided　　☐ Double sided

☐ Single density　☐ Double density　　☐ High density

Operating system_____

Version _____

Word processor program _____

Version _____

Imported maths/science program _____

Version _____

Graphics program _____

Version _____

Files have been saved in the following format

Text: _____

Figures: _____

Maths: _____

GORDON AND BREACH PUBLISHERS　　•　　**HARWOOD ACADEMIC PUBLISHERS**